Tarot

The History, Meaning, and Use of the Cards for Meditation and Divination

Written By Anne Burton

Tarot: The History, Meaning, and Use of the Cards   by *Anne Burton*

Tarot

The History, Meaning, and Use of the Cards for Meditation and Divination

Copyright © 2016 by Anne Burton

All rights reserved.

Printed in the United States of America. No part of this book may be used or reproduced in any manner whatsoever without written permission except in the case of brief quotations embodied in critical articles and reviews.

First Edition

Cover Designed by Heidi Milliken

Printed on acid-free paper

Library of Congress Control No: 2016958626

ISBN: 9781936533879

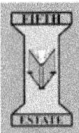

Fifth Estate 2016

Tarot: The History, Meaning, and Use of the Cards   by *Anne Burton*

Table of Contents

Introduction	7
History of the Tarot	9
Methods of Meditation	26
Methods of Divination	29
Major Arcana	42
Minor Arcana	115
Swords	119
Pentacles	146
Wands	173
Cups	201
How To Use A Deck of Playing Cards	229
Meaning of the Symbols of Tarot	247
Conclusion	253

Tarot: The History, Meaning, and Use of the Cards   by *Anne Burton*

Introduction

There arose in the fourteenth century a system of moral and spiritual teachings, a system that was used as a game and guide, a system that was steeped in the symbols and icons of Kings, clergy, courts, and the art of Renaissance Europe, a symbolism so powerful that it continues to teach us today. This tool is the Tarot. Although the first common use of the Tarot was as a game, shortly after its creation in approximately 1350, Tarot, or its predecessor, was adopted by monks to help them remember the moral code, to see the various sides of human nature, and to grow in their spiritual lives. What was it that the contemplative brothers saw in the Tarot? What universal truths did they learn from the cards? What spiritual insights are held in the pictures and symbols? How do these truths correspond to the Scriptures, which the monks attached to the cards? We will attempt to re-establish connections between the Tarot and the wisdom of the Scriptures. We will look into the various meanings of each card, and we will study the use of Tarot in acquiring a deeper knowledge of our past and present and future.

In this book we will elucidate the spiritual, Scriptural, and moral guidelines contained in the cards. We will explain how to use the cards in the areas of divination and personal meditation. We will look at the evolution of the cards from gaming to spiritual meditation and looking into future events. The history of Tarot will be discussed. How the cards became a parlor game and later a device of divination will be traced through social and religious change. Information and details will be given on how to divine the past, present, and future as we explore the use of the cards in modern society. From the year 1300 to today, this book bridges the gap and brings back to us the wisdom lost so long ago.

It is not the mind that moves the oracle. The Tarot kindly performs for both those amassed and bereft of the science of the mind. The oracle is moved by time itself. That thing, like the ocean tide, that ties all things, living and not, together into the dance and rhythm of synchronicity.

The tide is discerned by the swaying rushes, the wind by a bending bough and the tides of time by the oracle of the cards. Each moment contains a distinct imprint. Each can be reflected in the cards.

History of the Tarot

The exact origin of the Tarot is somewhat uncertain, but that has not stopped theories and myths to abound. Many believe the roots to be in ancient Egypt with the builders of the pyramids. Others think that the cards sprang from the worshipers of Thoth, the Egyptian god of writing, naming, magic, and equilibrium. In addition to these theories, there are those who link the cards back to the ancient Hebrews or to various mystery religions of Babylon and Chaldea. However, all traces fade with time and all connections become tenuous at best. The connections are usually made through myth, legend or conjecture.

The facts borne by history are that the cards appeared in the area of Italy and France at approximately 1300 A.D. At this period of time, card games appeared which were used for gambling, divination, and moral lessons. In 1332, King Alfonse XI of Italy banned the cards for the purpose of gaming or gambling. It is believed this was because he was frustrated by his inability to tax the money changing hands. In spite of being banned, the deep symbolism contained the cards kept them alive as a tool for inner guidance until today.

In 1377, a monk writes of a series of cards used by the brothers in his monastery, and adds that the cards may also be used as a moral guide. The brothers used the cards as a reminder of both the pitfalls and the pathway through the spiritual life.

The Tarot, or its predecessor, was used for three purposes, as mentioned in sermons by two different monks. The purposes were gaming, divination, and the teaching of moral lessons. By 1460 the Tarot had fallen into disrepute among the established church, possibly due to an edict from King Alfonse XI which made gambling with the Tarot illegal. It was at this time that a Franciscan friar preached a sermon on gaming, or gambling, in which Tarot was mentioned. The friar considered the cards "base." This seems to be an example of how politics shapes religion. In spite of the King's wishes, which may have been to keep the Tarot away from commoners, the popularity of Tarot could not be stopped by any reversal on the part of the local churches. Although its use in the monasteries ceased, the Tarot was to become a well known path of inner guidance and divination. Indeed, this attribute of the cards would become so strong as to totally eclipse the more mundane "gaming" aspect that the good friar held in such contempt.

The first appearance of Tarot cards, or cards resembling the modern Tarot deck, can be dated to and located with reasonable precision. Dates can be narrowed down to within a decade or two, and the location can be narrowed to within a few hundred miles.

European playing cards were an adaptation of cards brought from the Middle East. One of Europe's greatest civilizations - Moorish Spain - was flourishing at the time, and there was a great deal of intellectual exchange occurring between Europe and the Middle East. The Islamic Mamluk cards from the Middle East had suits of Cups,

Swords, Coins, and Sticks or Staves, as well as Courts consisting of a King and two Servants to the King.

The idea of Tarot, considered a type of playing card, probably evolved from the playing cards of the Islamic culture. Tarot adds the Fool, the Trumps (a set of cards depicting strengths, weaknesses, and virtues), and a set of Queens to the system. Some time before 1480, the French introduced cards with the now-familiar suits of Hearts, Clubs, Spades, and Diamonds. The earlier suits are still preserved in the Tarot in Italian and Spanish playing cards.

We know that playing cards were mentioned in Europe at about 1375. Records show that in 1392 Jacquemin Gringonneur was paid to paint three decks of cards for Charles VI. These were probably playing cards. However, it is interesting to note that the appearance of cards in general began to appear in the first part of the twelfth century. There is a distinction made between "playing cards" and the Tarot. This is actually a false distinction, in that the Tarot was a card game using a "trump and take" type of rule.

As general acceptance grew into preference, cards began to be the game of choice, supplanting dice in popularity. Because of this the cards of the time had 56 cards in the deck. We can see the evolution of dice and cards by noting that in the 10th century Bishop Wibold recommended the use of a dice game as a spiritual exercise. The game associated 56 clerical virtues with the 56 outcomes of three dice. At the end of the game, the players must exemplify the virtues for the rest of the day. Thierry Depaulis says, "Wibold was bishop of Cambrai (northern France) in the 10th century. He devised a complicated dice game called 'Ludus regularis seu clericalis' which was described in a Chronicle written in the following years. (This Chronicle was later edited and published in 1615). There is a long entry on the game in Jean-Marie L'hôte's Dictionnaire des Jeux de Société (1996)."

Gertrude Moakley mentioned Wibold's game in connection with the number of cards in a Tarot deck, "Why are there fifty-six suit cards, and why are there twenty-one trumps? The answer is found when we remember that cards, as a game of chance, replaced dice almost completely. In the dice games which use three dice, there are fifty-six possible throws, and with two dice twenty-one." The Fool card with no number or the number zero would be added to bring the total number of trump cards to twenty-two. This is the same number of letters in the Hebrew alphabet. The game of the time was called "Triumph".

The new concept of playing cards spawned the idea of the Tarot. Around 1420 references to cards with allegorical pictures appear. In the 1440's Triumph cards had evolved and a deck resembling Tarot began to appear. In 1440's the king requested a set of cards be made for the royal courts.

The Tarot was invented to be a game, but that the game was "smart", philosophically coherent and with a scholar's attention to numerical and theological principles.

Tarot cards were originally used for playing a card game called "tarocchi", and had nothing to do with foretelling the future. The Major Arcana cards or Trump cards did hold secret symbolic meanings for Sufis, who influenced the Kabala. The Kabala is related to the Hebrew alphabet, which has 22 letters. Each letter corresponds to a number and a virtue, weakness, or spiritual state.

The early Italian Renaissance was a time of great intellectual diversity and activity. Astrology, Pythagorean philosophy, and other viewpoints modern society now considers to be of the occult, lived side by side with Christian thought and all thrived. It should be remembered king and priest alike had their astrologers. All of these converging thoughts left their mark on the design of the Tarot. Thus, it should be remembered that all of the symbolism of the Tarot are closely analogous to the conventional Christian culture of the time. The Tarot decks were very ornate and contained pictures of the most basic human situations and virtues. The cards were used, not only for playing, but as meditation and reminders of spiritual and life lessons. Sermons were preached by monks about the lessons taught within the pictures of the cards. These pictures emulated the Christian world of 12th through 15th century Europe.

We do not know what lead to the use of the special group of symbols on the cards. Most are found in the art of the Italian Renaissance. Many are symbols of the states, conditions, and virtues of man. These symbols, such as Temperance, Death, or Judgment were placed on playing cards by Italian artists early in the 15th century. The designers seemed to have followed some prearranged plan of numbering and ordering the cards, but the reason has been lost to history.

The interest in the game grew quickly and gambling soon followed as wagers were placed on games. References to playing cards and ordinances enacted by cities and kings were instituted prohibiting gambling. As the kings began to oppose gambling and therefore the Tarot, the clergy followed suit. Sermons of clerics once expressing support for the ideals within the cards now turned to opposition. Sermons and lessons against the cards soon followed the kings' edicts.

The legal prohibitions against playing cards became stricter until in 1529 in Worchester, England card playing was commonly prohibited, with exceptions made including the twelve days of Christmas. The Bishop of Worchester, Hugh Latimer, preached a sermon on the Sunday before Christmas, comparing the game of Triumph (not Tarot) to the triumph of Christ. "And whereas you are about to celebrate Christmas in playing at cards, I intend, by God's grace, to deal unto you Christ's cards, wherein you shall perceive Christ's rule. The game that we shall play at shall be called the Triumph, which, if it be well played at, he that dealeth shall win; the players shall likewise win; and the standers and lookers upon shall do the same, insomuch that there is no man willing to play at this triumph with these cards but they shall be all winners and no losers."

The prohibitions against the cards, lead by the rulers, may have had more to do with their inability to track and tax the transfer of money than with any moral concerns.

We know that other Tarot-like sets of picture cards were made: the Tarocchi of Mantegna, with no suit cards but 50 trump-like cards of allegorical figures arranged in a hierarchy made explicit by a numbering and lettering scheme; the Sola-Busca, in which the subjects of the trump cards are completely changed, but the deck otherwise retains its structure, and finally, the Minchiate, which expands the trumps by the addition of signs of the zodiac, four elements, and missing virtues. We know Minchiate was a popular trick-taking game, very similar to Tarot, for several centuries. We have no direct references on what the Mantegna was used for.

The pictures within the Tarot were derived from various art, people, and beliefs of the time. In the 1300's Gertrude Moakley wrote about the Popess card in the Visconti-Sforza deck: "Her religious habit shows that she is of the Umilata order, probably Sister Manfreda, a relative of the Visconti family who was actually elected Pope by the small Lombard sect of the Guglielmites. Their leader, Guglielma of Bohemia, had died in Milan in 1281. The most enthusiastic of her followers believed that she was the incarnation of the Holy Spirit, sent to inaugurate the new age of the Spirit prophesied by Joachim of Flora. They believed that Guglielma would return to earth on the Feast of Pentecost in the year 1300 and that the male dominated Papacy would then pass away, yielding to a line of female popes."

"In preparation for the event, they elected Sister Manfreda the first of the Popesses, and several wealthy families of Lombardy provided at great cost the sacred vessels they expected her to use when she said Mass in Rome at the Church of Santa Maria Maggiore. Naturally, the Inquisition exterminated this new sect, and the 'Popess' was burned at the stake in the autumn of 1300. Later, the Inquisition proceeded against Matteo Visconti, the first Duke [imperial vicar?] of Milan, for his very slight connections with the sect."

In 1395 in the town of Milan, Italy, the Roman Emperor Wenceslaus appointed Giangaleazzo Visconti the first Duke of Milan, (for the price of 100,000 florins). "The formal coronation of Giangaleazzo as Duke of Milan took place on a Sunday morning, September 5, 1395, at the square in front of the ancient basilica of San Ambrogio.... Thus, the title, imperial vicar of Milan, was replaced by the title of Duke...." This was later to be reflected in heraldry included on Visconti Tarot decks.

Whether within the Popess card or the Heraldry of the Duke of Milan, the Tarot began to take on a political and spiritual commentary of the times.

In 1450, the newly installed Duke of Milan, Francesco Sforza, wrote a letter requesting the purchase of several packs of Triumph cards for use at court at special occasions. Instead of the ordinary suits of Swords, Coins, Staves, and Cups, the new deck was to have suits representing virtues, riches, virginities, and pleasures. The suit signs were appropriately birds: eagles, phoenixes, turtles, and / or doves, or possibly turtledoves. Each suit also had four cards higher than Kings, depicted as classical deities. This was apparently an early exploration into the idea of "trumps"; whereas, the regular suit cards have no power over cards of different suits, the sixteen deities have an internal ordering that bypasses their suit assignments and determines which card wins over others.

The letter mentions a deck of Triumph cards and playing cards, indicating there were two different decks in use at the time. Playing cards were the Duke's second choice, to be purchased in case Triumph cards were unavailable. This shows the Tarot had "evolved" to a point where it was being used as a playing deck for a game similar to bridge and available to the general public. However, it does not mean the cards were not also used for instructional or esoteric purposes, but it does show the primary use at this time was for gaming. These facts seem to be supported by evidence of the oldest surviving cards, which art historians have dated to the reign of Filippo Maria Visconti, Duke of Milan from 1412 to 1447.

In Strasbourg, Germany, 1502, a Franciscan monk named Thomas Murner published an educational deck with 16 suits teaching the Law, based on the Institutes of Justinian. Thus began the fecund tradition of educational cards. "With the intention of increasing interest in reading, I have tried to counter immoral games through this extremely uplifting game of the imperial institutes and I would esteem myself fortunate if I should have succeeded in restricting that which is bad by that which is good." A related book, Chartiludium Institute Summarie, was published decades later, in 1528. A second game from Murner, with 12 suits teaching logic, was published in 1507. (Dummett gives dates of 1509 and 1515 for these two decks, respectively.) In addition to his inventions of the suits, both decks included five "standard" suits: Bells, Acorns, Hearts, Shields, and Crowns.

Although the Court Cards seemed to carry messages of personality traits and were used in poetry in the late 1500's, evidence of divinatory meanings assigned to Tarot cards did not appear clearly until 1700 in Bologna, Italy. It is commonly understood that ordinary playing cards were connected with divination as early as 1487, so it is suspected Tarot was as well. From the 1790's with Etteilla's deck we find Tarot design being modified specifically to reflect divinatory and esoteric meanings.

It wasn't until 1589 in the records of a trial in Venice that Tarot may have been associated with witchcraft...coming approximately 150 years after the appearance of the Tarot.

Not until the late 1700's did the first occult writers discuss the Tarot. For the first 350 years of its history, the Tarot was not mentioned in any of the many books on occult or magical philosophy. Following 1781, occult interest in Tarot blossomed and the Tarot became an integral part of occult philosophy. It is interesting that occult practices were not seen to be the same as witchcraft even in that period of time. Occult knowledge points to a hidden and deeper knowledge, whereas witchcraft was taken to be a contract and servitude with Satan.

A short article on the Tarot was published in Court de Gébelin's Le Monde Primitif (1781), was the first to write of a connection between the Hebrew letters and the cards. Court de Gébelin also mentioned the idea in passing in his own essay.

In card games, the 22 Major Arcana cards were trump cards, and the 56 Minor Arcana cards in four suits are similar to today's standard deck of 52 cards in four suits. The Tarot added Queens, Knights, and Pages to the Court Cards.

All the surviving Triumph cards from the 15th century are from northern Italy. By the early 16th century, use of the cards had certainly spread to France. Around 1530 the word Tarocchi (Italian ancestor of the French Tarot) first appears. The change in name was due to a change in playing tactics. The game of Triumphs could be played with an ordinary playing-card deck, if the players, as in the game of bridge, declared a particular suit to serve as "trumps" at the beginning of the game or the hand. Hence "triumphs" ("trumps") became an ambiguous term for any card called out for the purpose. Thus the word Tarocchi came to be used for those trumps used in the special deck of the Tarot, although its etymology remains uncertain.

As the cards breached the boundaries of culture and language they spread, and so the names of the cards change and evolve with various cultures and languages.

Between the Italian beginnings and the modern English, most have remained generally the same. Some have not.

The Fool card is an example of how culture and language has swayed the card. The Fool card was once known as the Jester; the Magician card was also called the Juggler, Bagatella, Bagatino, and Bagatto. (Bagatella means someone using a wand, in the sense of a conjurer or parade performer). The Chariot was once Carro Triumphale, Carro, and Triumphal Chariot. The Hermit was Gobbo, Vecchio, Tempo, Hunchback, Old Man, or Time. The Hanged Man was Impiccato, Traditore, and Traitor. Likewise, Chariot is probably an abbreviation of Triumphal Chariot, a title that associates the card more strongly with the triumph processions.

Early Italian cards depict the Last Judgment scene but the title Judgment is never used. Instead the Angel is the name of the card and the focus of the card is not as "inevitable and grim."

The Hanged Man is called the Traitor. A traitor was depicted hung upside down as a means of propaganda. It had nothing to do with the modern interpretation of surrendering to God as Peter did.

The following titles and sequence are from a French deck dating from the late 1500's:

Fool; Bagatto; Popess; Empress; Emperor; Pope; Love; Chariot; Justice; Old Man; Wheel; Fortitude; Traitor; Death; Temperance; Devil; Fire; Star; Moon; Sun; Angel; World.

To understand the meanings of the Tarot, one must keep in mind the time and place of the invention of the cards. Europe in the 1400's through 1500's was driven by the Church and the King. If one focuses on Europe in the Middle Ages, the Tarot takes on a deeper and more direct meaning.

Jesuit Claude François Menestrier of Lyon, France wrote in 1704 of the interpretation, or re-interpretation of the four suits as social allegories. "Hearts represented men of the Church; Diamonds the Merchants; Clubs were the symbols of Peasantry; and Spades that of the 'Noblesse d'epee'. ...these meanings were familiar to Court de Gébelin and the comte de Mellet." "Court Cards, he says, represent the nobility, Hearts the ecclesiastics, their place being in the c(h)oeur, ('choir'); pikes, (Spades) represent the nobility; carreaux (paving-tiles) the bourgeoisie; and trefoils the peasantry."

The English derived their playing card designs from the French, so when the Order of the Golden Dawn and other British occultists were searching around for things that looked mysterious, Tarot cards filled the bill nicely. The Golden Dawn was concerned about the occult or "new age" uses of the cards and began to alter the cards for that purpose. The Free Masons shared many symbols with the Golden Dawn and looking into the Tarot one clearly sees the influence of A.E Waite's Free Mason connections. As the purpose was better defined, the cards took on qualities better suited for meditation, inspiration, and fortune telling.

The cards used in this book are from the Waite-Rider of Waite-Smith deck. The Waite-Smith deck was created in 1909, making it a relative newcomer in the almost-600-year history of the Tarot. A. E. Waite was a prominent member of the Hermetic Order of the Golden Dawn. The deck owes much of its symbolism to that group and represents a departure from the earlier French tradition. The artist, Pamela Colman Smith, contributed her own vision, especially in the innovative creation of fully illustrated scenes for the Minor Arcana. For many years, the Waite-Smith deck was the only one readily available in the U.S., so became familiar to generations of Tarot readers.

Today, the Tarot deck consists of two major divisions. There are 56 cards, called the Minor Arcana (arcane means mysterious or hidden), and 22 cards, called the Major Arcana. The Minor Arcana is broken down into cards from Ace to 10 and the Court Cards made up of the Page, Knight, Queen, and King. There are four suits of Minor Arcana: Cups, Swords, Wands, and Pentacles. In some decks, Wands are called Batons and Pentacles are called Coins or Disks, but the meaning and appearance remain unchanged.

The Major Arcana consists of 22 cards. They are numbered from 1 to 21 with a card called the Fool, which is numbered as 0 or left completely unnumbered. The Major Arcana have no suit. In the Tarot, the Major Arcana is used to exemplify the important conditions or stages in life. As an expression of this circle of life and human growth, it seems logical to keep the Fool unnumbered since the circle connects and reconnects through it. In keeping with the ancient emphasis on the Major Arcana, there will be additional more specific information provided about these cards and their lessons in spiritual growth. Part of the thrust of this work will be to bring back to focus the tie between the Major Arcana and spiritual guideposts in the human life.

From its origins far back in the mists of history until today, the Tarot has continued to be honed and sharpened. The symbolism has been tweaked and refined, finally yielding the systems millions have come to trust.

The Tarot is not some unfathomable, super-spiritual tool. As a matter of fact, its primary purpose was never intended to be divination. The cards themselves cannot tell the future. They can see no more clearly nor any further than our own subconscious mind. The Cards can and will reveal and focus the power of our minds and allow us to use our own abilities to "intuit" our inner psyche and our future. Today, the Tarot's two main uses are first, to focus the subconscious mind and whatever powers it may contain, and secondly, to show us a path for personal growth so that we may see where we stand on our way. In short, we have all of the knowledge and power already within us. The Tarot simply focuses our minds and spirits through the deep symbolism of the cards.

For years, many Tarot practitioners have made the cards out to be something unreachable and not to be understood by the masses; as if the Tarot only works for those who have special powers. This is, no doubt, to make themselves out to be more than they really are. Anyone can use the Tarot. The oracle will work its magic for all. Most of the symbols are not hidden or mysterious. They are simply archaic and outdated. They were a consequence of Europe in the twelfth through fourteenth centuries. Yet, having understood the meanings of the cards, we must look past them to find how it applies to ourselves here and now.

As strange as it sounds, the objective in using any occult tool is to come to a point where the tool is no longer needed. Having the answers already within us, we should eventually be able to focus out intuitions without the symbolism of the tool and one day leave it behind. Until that day, use this wonderful system. Bathe in its symbolism. Let it teach you. Let it become a part of you until, one day, you transcend the teacher.

Methods of Meditation

"Shape Of My Heart" (Lyrics by Sting)

He deals the cards as a meditation
And those he plays never suspect
He doesn't play for the money he wins
He don't play for respect

He deals the cards to find the answer
The sacred geometry of chance
[Studio version:] The hidden law of a probable outcome
[Live version:] The hidden laws of a probable outcome
The numbers lead a dance

I know that the spades are the swords of a soldier
I know that the clubs are weapons of war
I know that diamonds mean money for this art
But that's not the shape of my heart

He may play the Jack of diamonds
He may lay the Queen of spades
He may conceal a King in his hand
While the memory of it fades...

The One Card Meditation

First, take all Major Arcana out of the deck. These will be the only cards we will use for this exercise.

Use only the Major Arcana. Clear your mind and shuffle the cards well. Select one card. Look up the meaning and scriptures attached to this card. Meditate on the meanings, both positive and negative, attached to the card. Find and focus on the positive traits within you. Fell that trait and energy in you. Make it bigger and better in you. Practice it all day. Find the negative traits attached to the card within you. Allow yourself to see how these traits held you back. Feel the traits and feel how much you want them out of your life. Recognize them, abhor them and eliminate them. Hold back the negative. Accentuate the positive. Above all, recognizing traits and being willing to change are the first steps in being a better person.

The Three Card Meditation

Like the "One Card Meditation," the "Three-Card Meditation technique uses only the Major Arcana. Shuffle and select three cards. The first represents your past, the second card represents your present, and the third card represents your future. These cards are not only general indications of events, they are signposts to your emotional and mental disposition. Therefore, they point toward positive and negative traits, which will indicate strengths and weaknesses in your personality within various situations. This point needs to be stressed. Certain strengths and weaknesses make themselves known under certain circumstances. We may be strong one day and weak the next. The differences usually come down to circumstances, which act as triggers. Many of these we are blind to. This method helps us see the connections.

Methods of Divination

Before each reading, turn all the cards upright so they face in the same direction. Pick up the cards and clear your mind. If you are interested in one particular situation or question, concentrate specifically on it. If you want a general reading, keep your mind clear. Synchronicity will do the rest. Time, and all of the unnamed qualities it possesses, binds us together with all things around us ... just as we see things happen in patterns, or we speak of a friend and he calls, or we miss someone and suddenly run into them. Time, like the tide of the ocean, washes things in and out of our lives. As we shuffle the cards, cutting them over and over again, the same essence of the time we are in, is shuffled into the cards. These feelings will be related to the question or situation at hand.

As you lay the cards out in the pattern you will be shown, you must let the symbolism of the cards speak to you. The cards have certain meanings, but they also speak directly to the subconscious mind. You will become aware of this connection with fleeting ideas and feelings as you study the cards. These feelings will be related to the question or situation at hand.

Let us begin. As you cut the deck over and over again, randomly select three cards. Without looking at them, turn these cards upside down. When a card is upside down it is said to be "Inverted". Reinsert these inverted cards back into the deck. Continue to cut the cards until they feel as if they are shuffled completely and ready to be read.

Fourteen cards will be laid out in the specific pattern shown here:

(11)   (3)   (10)

(12)   (1)   (9)

(13)   (6)   (2)   (5)   (8)

(14)   (4)   (7)

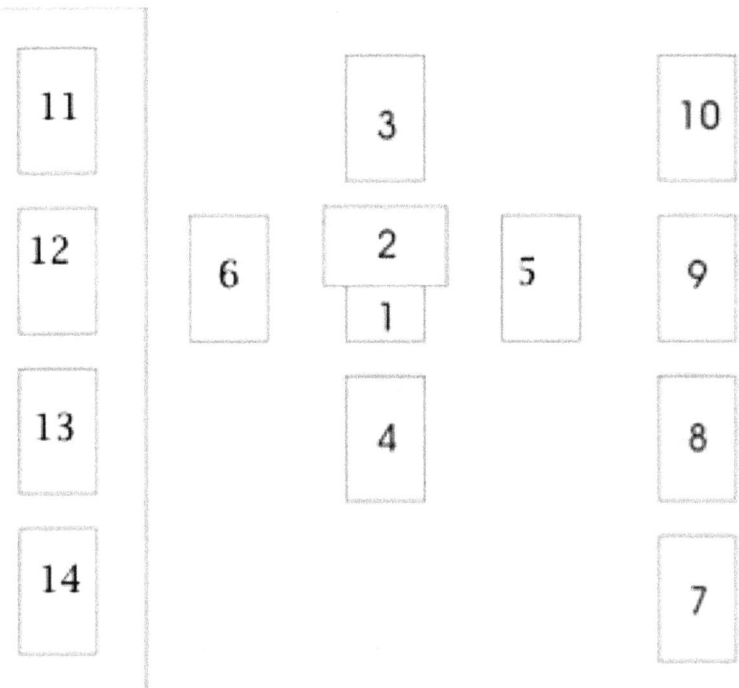

Position (1) refers to present influence - the atmosphere in which you are working and living.

Position (2) refers to the immediate obstacle just ahead.

Position (3) refers to the specific goals, objectives, and what is possible on this path.

Position (4) is a broad picture of the past and how you got to this place.

Position (5) refers to events which have just past.

Position (6) refers to events in the near future.

Position (7) refers to the person being read. It is their position, attitude, and perspective in regard to the question.

Position (8) refers to the environment. It is the interaction between the person and those close to you.

Position (9) refers to the hopes or fears surrounding the question.

Position (10) refers to the final outcome of the question.

Position (11) refers to the state of mind or internal posture regarding the question.

Position (12) refers to emotions and feelings about the question.

Position (13) refers to the circumstance that will come about which will cause the final outcome. It may be referred to as the doorway to the future.

Position (14) refers to the final outcome. It contains additional information about card (10).

Reading the Spread

Reading the cards can be compared to reading a map. Any good map has its cardinal points of north, south, east, and west. The spread has its cardinal points also, but they are set in time instead of space. Just as when reading a map, confusion arises if compass points are ignore; in reading the cards, the time line cannot be ignored. The four compass points of the cards are the past, the present, the future, and the possibilities. To give a good, clear and accurate reading, it is best to group the cards into these four categories. After the cards are grouped accordingly, the story the cards wish to tell will spring to life.

As with any map, there are landscapes. In life experiences, there are both internal and external landscapes to take into account. External landscapes are made up of events and situations. Internal landscapes consist of emotions, hopes, fears, and postures. Emotions fall into the obvious categories of love, hate, fear, happiness, sadness, loneliness, and satiation. Internal postures may best be described as ways of approaching or looking at an event or situation. Some of these approaches are determination, apathy, patience, exacerbation, reluctance, and resignation.

As the lay out shows, card positions four and five relate to the past, therefore it is best to start any reading from these cards.

Position (4) is the foundation of the reading. This position gives a broad glimpse into the past events that brought the person to this point. It is a hint at the question being asked by the seeker.

Positions (1), (7), and (8) give insight into what the questioner is experiencing in the present.

The future is told by positions (6), (10), (13), and (14).

This leaves possibilities, things that could happen if the present path is followed to its completion. This is summed up in position (3) - this position may also be read as the person's aims or goals.

Having thus divided the positions, and the cards into the positions, we are now prepared to start from the past and follow the cards into the future, step by step. Along the way, we can also help the seeker, be it ourselves or another, understand the hopes, fears, aims, goals objectives, frame of mind, and even possibilities of the path being taken.

Begin with the card in position (4). Let it speak to you of the past, which has brought the seeker thus far. This position indicates the general and far-ranging past and is the more distant past position.

Next, read the card in position (5). It is the past that has just occurred - the immediate past.

Following on the timeline are positions (1), (2), and (7).

Position (1) represents the present event or situation.

Position (2) defines the obstacles or positive influences surround the present experiences. Cards one and two combine to show the present position of the person on the time map. They represent what situation or event is transpiring now, as well as anything that fate is handing over.

Position (2) is the magic mirror into what fate is doing with the present conditions. There are runs of good luck, bad luck, and all things in between; however, the most important is that position (2) discloses from which direction, circumstance or person fate will intervene.

We then add position (7) to the mix. It is a cross-over position having the potential to comment on present position, as well as attitude and perspective. Since this card bridges the gap between the inner and outer landscapes, it would flow well to read the rest of the cards connected with this mode.

We now examine position (9) which speaks of the hopes or fears surrounding the situation; position (11) which deals with the emotional response to the situation; and position (12) which is the mind-set or the internal position being taken.

We have now visualized the seeker's present state; however, the item which affects us almost as much as our own mood, is the mood of our family and friends.

Position (8) tells us how our closest friends and family are reacting and feeling in the current situation. This knowledge can be of great importance to the seeker and is truly the icing on the cake on our view of the present.

Now we move our attention to the future. The doorway to the future is found in position (13). This is the event that is expected to transpire before the future unfolds on our path. Because of this link to the future, this card also hints at the future. It sits between the present and position (6).

Position (6) is the near future. Plainly, it is the next major event on this path.

Look now to the card in position (3). It is the seeker's aims, goals, objectives, or what is possible given the present path. It can serve as a warning of things to come based on the present course taken to its final outcome.

Lastly, we examine positions (10) and (14). Position (10) is the final outcome and the answer to the seeker's question or his probably destiny within approximately the next three months.

Position (14) serves as a minor commentary for card (10). It supplies more information regarding the final events of the subsequent three-month path. It is important to understand that the cards do not normally give us more than a three-month window into the future.

The position of the near future card (6) is the story as it will unfold with the next month.

The position (10) card reveals the future to the three-month mark. It is not uncommon for the (10) and (14) cards to tell a story of a balance, stagnation or unrevealed future. This means simply that the final outcome is more than three months in the future; or that the path is unsettled because the seeker has not made a firm commitment to a particular path. In these cases, it is best to return in a week and inquire of the cards once again.

Remember, begin with the past, then read the present with all its emotions and attitudes, and finish by charting the course of the future. By that time, the fog will have cleared and the final outcome should be very visible.

Always keep in mind that our future depends on our path, our attitude, and our reactions to the past and present events. Changing our attitude, reaction, and frame of mind will alter our future.

A Quicker Read

Three Card Method

Using the entire deck, shuffle the deck with one of the following set of questions in mind.

SITUATION
Past / Present / Future
The nature of your problem / The cause / The solution
Current situation / Obstacle / Advice
Situation / Action / Outcome

RELATIONSHIP
You / The other person / The relationship

Your position in the relationship / Their position in the relationship / Where the relationship is heading

What brings you together / What pulls you apart / What needs your attention

DECISIONS
Opportunities / Challenges / Outcome
Chose between first solution / second solution / How to choose

YOURSELF

Mind / Body / Spirit

Material state / Emotional state / Spiritual state

Your path / your position / what it takes to reach your potential

The Simple Celtic Cross

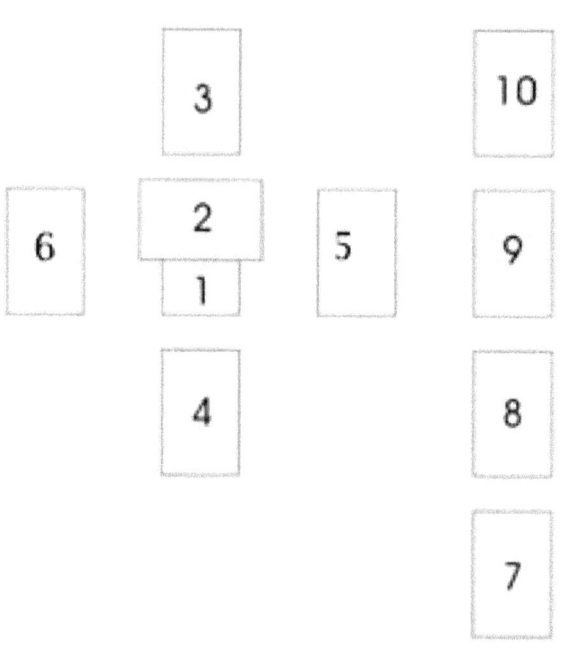

As you lay out the cards say, "1 - this represents you (This covers you). 2- This crosses you. 3 - This is your aim. 4 - This is your foundation. 5 This is behind you. 6 - This is ahead of you. 7 - This is what you think. 8 - This is who is close to you. 9 - This is how you feel. 10 - this is the outcome."

Position (1) refers to present influence - the atmosphere in which you are working and living.

Position (2) refers to the immediate obstacle just ahead.

Position (3) refers to the specific goals, objectives, and what is possible on this path.

Position (4) is a broad picture of the past and how you got to this place.

Position (5) refers to events which have just past.

Position (6) refers to events in the near future.

Position (7) refers to the person being read. It is their position, attitude, and perspective in regard to the question.

Position (8) refers to the environment. It is the interaction between the person and those close to you.

Position (9) refers to the hopes or fears surrounding the question.

Position (10) refers to the final outcome of the question.

Major Arcana

The Major Arcana represents the more sweeping or important decisions of life. They also contain, in their symbolism, life lessons and spiritual signposts. They comment on our moral evolution and give guidance to the next stage on our path.

When a Major Arcana appears in a future position, it is interpreted as an event of importance, which will be difficult to avoid.

The monks of the 1300's used the Major Arcana to teach lessons of a Biblical or spiritual nature. We will look into this aspect of these cards with much greater depth than the others. The Biblical connections will be revealed and along with these life lessons will come a deep, abiding understanding of the true meaning and purpose of Tarot cards.

For each card, the commentary is divided into several sections. The mundane meaning of the card is presented according to its orientation, either upright or inverted. The next section gives insight to the card's meaning in a reading. It is followed by a list of comments based on the usual concerns such as job, romance, resources, and possibilities. The final section for each card is labeled "spiritual signpost." This section will yield insight into the true, deeper meaning of the card. It will trace an unmistakable path from the beginning to the end of man's spiritual journey and the pitfalls along the way. With the understanding of this section, the full meaning of each card will be revealed.

The Magician - Card 1 of the Major Arcana

Meaning if card is upright - Builder, artist, manager. An originator of new ideas or inventions. New modes. Bringing ideas into existence. Willpower, action, tenacity, follow-through, ability. Manifesting organizational skills. How will you accomplish your goals? By your sheer will!

Meaning if card is inverted - Selfish, manipulating. Incorrect use of power, ineptitude. A project fails, no follow-through, Lack of will, disquiet, confusion, ill-intent.

In the reading - The person represented by this card is a willful, creative or dynamic person. He is creative and logical, using both left and right side of his brain. The cards that follow will show if he has been successful. In the reverse, this card may indicate he tends to be selfish or vengeful, possibly weak willed.

Job and endeavors - Give it all you've got and great things will happen. Practice, study, and application bring things to pass. With the Ace of Pentacles - new starts with resources, job, business venture. With the 8 of Pentacles - new training or employment.

Romance and marriage - Power, sexuality, and assertiveness increases. With the Ace of Cups -joy and fertility.

Resources - Time to direct your resources toward your goals. With an Ace of Wands - birth, invention, enterprise. With the 6 of Wands - victory.

Environment, path, and possibilities - Focus and determination yields success. With the Ace of Swords – triumph; with the World or the Sun cards, success. With the Devil - hidden agendas, strange occurrences.

Spiritual signpost - On the path, this card is one of breaking the inertia and status quo by the application of organization and willpower. A wish does not make things come true, but it is the point of origin. From there willpower brings things into being. If you learn to focus your mind and energies, there is nothing that is not possible on the physical plane. That is not where this card ends, however.

The Magician card is also known as the Juggler in other decks. This symbolism adds new insight into its meaning. Namely, the realization that all which can be accomplished in our physical world is trickery. The best we can hope for in this framework is to become accomplished in our meaningless or limited corporeal sphere. This card is the use of the mind and the will together with the epiphany that this is not all there is.

This glimpse sets the stage for the awakening and the use of the subconscious mind. This transition is seen clearest in intensive physical training. As the athlete makes his way toward perfection in form, he encounters limits as to what can be physically accomplished. At this point, a great frustration begins to brew within him. As he struggles he digs deeper and deeper into his psyche. A connection is made to that part of him that was previously inaccessible. Feeling, insights, and energies begins to emerge. He becomes a fully functioning person, operating on a spiritual as well as a physical level. He is now a priest in his own right - a force to be reckoned with. All you see is not all there is!

Ecc 1:14 - I have seen all the works that are done under the sun, and behold, it is all vanity (emptiness) and vexation of spirit.

Mat 28:18 - And Jesus came and spake unto them, saying, All power is given unto me in heaven and earth.

2 TI 1:7 - For God hath not given us the spirit of fear; but of power, and of love, and of a sound mind.

John 1:12 - But as many as received him, to them he gave power to become the sons of God, even to them that believed on his name: Which were born, not of blood, nor of the will of the flesh, nor of the will of man, but of God.

Luke 10:19 - Behold, I give unto you power to tread on serpents and scorpions, and over all the power of the enemy, and nothing shall by any means hurt you.

The High Priestess - Card 2 of the Major Arcana

Meaning if card is upright - Mystery and intuition come from the subconscious; spiritual enlightenment, emotions blend with logic, inner illumination, taking emotional chances. Sensual attraction taken to the limit; Passivity, femininity, and intuition. Mysteriously, she stirs your soul - a connection or attraction you don't understand; knowledge and intuition combined.

Meaning if card is inverted - A selfish and ruthless woman - indulgent, a gold-digger, interested in outward show. Filled with conceit and only surface knowledge. In a man's reading, this card means he must be careful not to be destroyed by such a woman.

In the reading - This interesting card contains a number of symbols, but the primary meanings concern the hidden matters suggested by the moon. Ideas through intuition. In a man's reading, the High Priestess suggests he will meet a woman he will be instantly attracted to. If the card is in the past, he has already met her. In reverse, the card indicates that a conceited, selfish woman is mixed up in the question asked. If the High Priestess is in a woman's cards, it shows her own nature.

It is worth more than a footnote to explain that the letters "J" and "B" on the pillars are referred to in the Bible. When speaking of the building of the temple of God, specifically the great temple of Solomon, the Bible reads:

2CH 3:17 And he reared up pillars before the temple ... and called the name of that one on the right JACHIN, and the name of the one on the left BOAZ.

The name Jachin means "founding" and Boaz means "strength." These are very strong names for what is a very feminine card and show the inner strength of the High Priestess.

Boaz is also the name of the man who saved Ruth from starvation and redeemed her from a life of abject poverty. He symbolizes a Christ-like figure in the Old Testament - a foreshadowing of the redeemer to come. In this view of this symbolism, we are looking at justice represented in Jachin, and mercy represented in Boaz. These two strong but opposing forces, which can only be meted out in a God who can see into the hearts of all people, are together as the symbolic support of the great temple. For mankind to act justly and with mercy is a noble aim indeed. Is it any wonder that ancient decks of cards refer to her as the "Popess?"

Job and endeavors - Go with your instinct. If reversed, delays and set backs are in store.

Romance and marriage - Follow your heart - romance and marriage are swift and sure. You will meet someone. If reversed, it is not meant to be.

Resources - Watch for change and fluctuation. Resources get better. If reversed - expect set backs and loss.

Environment, path, and possibilities - Pick your time to make your play. Don't go until you feel strong.

Spiritual signpost - The mind alone will not accomplish it all - the most important choices in life are made with insufficient data. You must trust your intuition. Open your heart and trust the spirit inside ... use that part of you opened by the Magician card.

Son 5:2 - I sleep, but my Heart waketh: it is the voice of my beloved that knocketh, saying, Open to me, my sister, my love, my dove, my undefiled: for my head is filled with dew, and my locks with the drops of the night.

Eze 11:19 - And I will give them one Heart, and I will put a new spirit within you; and I will take the stony Heart out of their flesh, and I will give them a Heart of flesh.

1 Sa 2:35 - And I will raise me up a faithful priest, that shall do according to that which is in mine Heart and in my mind: and I will build him a sure house; and he shall walk before mine anointed forever.

The Empress - Card 3 of the Major Arcana

Meaning if card is upright - Marriage, romance, fertility, birth, creativity. A balance of the yin and yang brings forth fruit. An open, straight forward character. Also wealth, contentment, a fruitful harvest, creative, self-expression. Earth-mother, nurturing, mothering.

Meaning if card is inverted - Infidelity, deceit, guile, poverty, emotional problems, introverted, or depressed. The inability to integrate contrasting feelings, also anti-social and unable to deal with people.

In the reading - This card represents pregnancy, fertility, creativity, and wealth. It may mean she recently has had or will have a child. If you are reading for a man, he will shortly be a father or have creative success. You can suggest he will have resources, possessions or a successful venture. With the High Priestess, the Empress card indicates a strong connection with the feminine nature.

Job and endeavors - Keep going. Things will take longer than you like, but there will be gain. If reversed, there will be cutbacks, a slowing down and hard times.

Romance and marriage – This is very good card - marriage, commitment, and children. If reversed, there may be difficulty getting pregnant or carrying a child. Romance or marriage postponed.

Resources - Investments are looking up; a yield is coming soon. If reversed - loss, withdrawal, market losses.

Environment, path, and possibilities - Everything is done that you can do - now sit and watch. If reversed, plans go wrong.

Spiritual signpost - Mother Mary? Probably. This card represents the ultimate mother image, the mother of God. When mind and heart are combined, the offspring is creativity. You must seek to keep the correct balance between head and heart. The heart dreams and does nothing. The mind has no soul. It takes both to be truly human. Mary accepted what God had in store for her.

Mar 10:7 - For this cause shall a man leave his father and mother, and cleave to his wife; And they twain shall be one flesh: so then they are no more twain, but one flesh.

Prov 31:10 Who can find a virtuous woman? for her price is far above rubies .11 The heart of her husband doth safely trust in her, so that he shall have no need of spoil. 12 She will do him good and not evil all the days of her life. 13 She seeketh wool, and flax, and worketh willingly with her hands. 14 She is like the merchants' ships; she bringeth her food from afar. 15 She riseth also while it is yet night, and giveth meat to her household, and a portion to her maidens. 16 She considereth a field, and buyeth it: with the fruit of her hands she planteth a vineyard. 17 She girdeth her loins with strength, and strengtheneth her arms. 18 She perceiveth that her merchandise is good: her candle goeth not out by night. 19 She layeth her hands to the spindle, and her hands hold the distaff. 20 She stretcheth out her hand to the poor; yea, she reacheth forth her hands to the needy.

The Emperor - Card 4 of the Major Arcana

Meaning if card is upright - Authority, fatherhood - you are a strong parent figure, a protector. Leadership, government, big business. Controlling in nature, an administrator, regulating, self-made, logical, reasonable. Definite strong male sexuality.

Meaning if card is inverted - Weak willed, loss of self-control, easily led, tied to the apron strings - a parent exerts too much influence; emotional immaturity, loss.

In the reading - Trouble, loss, scandal, resources are squandered. An authority figure, parent, a boss, police, judge or commanding officer. If reversed, watch for loss, loss of focus, injury or accident.

Job and endeavors - Be sure not to cross the boss or stretch the rules. Go by the book and all will be well. Inverted - reorganization.

Romance and marriage - Control is the issue - a parent/child, husband or father. Relationship is in need of attention.

Resources - Need to look ahead and plan for the long term.

Environment, path, and possibilities - Don't let your guard drop. Be on the offensive. Move first - the authority is watching.

Spiritual signpost - Increased understanding brings increased power, and power demands control of self. There is a difference between authority and a need to control. Others can give us authority, but we must take control. Therefore, control is intrusive and temporary; it must always be enforced if it is not willingly given. Control springs from an ego weakness, it is unbendable. Authority comes from force of personality. It is how others respond. This card urges along the line of authority. Take care of people, value their love and trust. Keep strong in convictions founded in love and others will give you authority. This card is the father image. It represents God the father, the paternal, protector, authority, giver of power, provider.

Luk 14:17 - And he said unto him, Well, thou good and faithful servant: because thou has been faithful in a very little, have thou authority over ten cities.

Luk 9:1- Then he called his twelve disciples together, and gave them power over all devils, and to cure diseases.

Mat 28:18 And Jesus came and spake unto them, saying, All power is given unto me in heaven and in earth.

The Hierophant- Card 5 of the Major Arcana

Meaning if upright - Education - A need to conform to old or outdated modes. An over-emphasis on being socially accepted. An outward show for the benefit of others. Pharisaic, hypocritical. Preference for the outer forms of religion that do not touch the soul. Preoccupied with what the neighbors think. When anything becomes a habit or ritual, the true, living, underlying meaning begins to die.

Liturgy instead of worship. Ritual instead of understanding. Habit instead of living in the moment.

Meaning if inverted - Unconventionality, unorthodoxy, superstitious counter culture. Illegal operations.

In a reading -You feel the need to conform to the moral and ethical constraints, even if you don't agree with them. Social pretense to please parents or the people down the street. If the Hierophant turns up in the past, this attitude is already characteristic of the person being read. But if the Hanged Man or other spiritual cards come up in the future, it is safe to predict that the present attitude will change to one of more openness to spiritual ideas. If inverted, this card indicates unconventionality and counter culture. There is a warning here that the person being read is delving into the occult or becoming superstitious.

Job and endeavors - Try to relax. Think in new ways. Try to be innovative. Fear of stepping out may hold you back. Pray, get path and possibilities, then move.

Romance and marriage - Confessions, commitment, vows. You may learn the difference between forgiving and forgetting.

Resources - Try to help those in need. It will come back to you.

Environment, path, and possibilities - You are not really in control. There are too many variables in the environment, so do the best you can and hold on. Things will settle soon.

Spiritual signpost - A once new enlightenment can become stale if we let it. We must remember from where we came and swear never to return to our ignorant roots. Day to day living can dull the spirit. Wake up and see things from a fresh perspective.

On the path of spiritual growth, this card is a warning sign. As we become established in life and reach our goals it is easy to forget where we came from. It is also easy to forget that fate has given us the opportunity to exploit. Outer show doesn't mean a thing. God judges the heart. How much we give, where we go to worship, what we wear, and with whom we are seen do not matter. The only thing that matters is our heart. Our anthem should always be: I am no more than the least of you.

In the earliest days of the Christian Church according to the Book of Acts, Chapter 2, there were no concepts, no New Testament, and no church buildings. The only guidance these new Christians had was God's spirit within them. Their faith was alive and new, inspired by the living God. Within three hundred years there was little need of faith or spirit. The church had grown up along with its doctrine, rules, and presumptuous authority. It claimed that man's salvation and enlightenment were in its hands. Living, working faith began to die as people put their faith in the church, instead of in the God it supposedly served. The Hierophant represents faith traded for ritual; living enlightenment exchanged for liturgy; living spirit left behind for the safety of habit.

Heb 7:19 For the law made nothing perfect, but the bringing in of a better hope did; by the which we draw nigh unto God.

Mat 26:59 Now the chief priest, and elders, and all the council, sought false witness to put him to death.

The Lovers - Card 6 of the Major Arcana

Meaning if upright - Choice between lust and love. (Agape' or Eros.) Vice and virtue. Temptation. The beginning of romance with choices made to be illicit or open. Harmony, inspiration from above. Romance or marriage uncontaminated by ego or selfish desire. Finding your complement. Lust or love satisfied. The apple of your eye.

Meaning if reversed - Infidelity. Jealousy. A need to control or consume. Quarrels over children. Wrong choice of the heart. The need to stabilize the emotions.

In a reading - This is a good and happy card. Usually it means the beginning of romance. It can also mean temptation and marriages. With a Queen card in the future there may be jealousy. When reversed, this card may mean there is in-law trouble, a sister or brother, or even a friend has caused an upset. With the Justice card – it concerns marriage, divorce or vows.

Job and endeavors - A reorganization. Romance and marriage and job and endeavors mix.

Romance and marriage - This is a good relationship. Things are right. Reversed - rebound, a one night stand. Lust not romance and marriage. Fights, breakups.

Resources - Join forces for more strength, but read the fine print.

Environment, path, and possibilities - Use tact, charm, sex appeal to scope things out. Size things up. Play it close to the chest.

Spiritual signpost - Is the Love agape' or Eros? Do you want to nurture and give, or do you want to consume or control? This is a turning point, or a reference mark. Is the love pure, or just lust? The aim here is agape'. With that love comes the wish to serve others, not to consume or control them.

Adam and Eve, once innocent and within the garden of Eden, talked to God daily, gave up this blissful state in order to know what was good and bad. Along with this knowledge came lust and sexual love. Innocence knows no passion, but passion is suffering. There is always something lost.

Son 2:4 He brought me to the banqueting house, and his banner over me was love.

Gen 29:20 And Jacob served seven years for Rachel; and they seemed unto him but a few days, for the love he had to her.

Gal 5:16 This I say then, Walk in the spirit, and ye shall not fulfill the lust of the flesh.

The Chariot - Card 7 of the Major Arcana

Meaning if upright - Will power, stubbornness; perseverance brings success. Victory through hard work. Triumph over an adversary or circumstances. Resources improve. Difficulties subside. A responsible nature. An ability to resist temptation. Travel. A true warrior is a balanced individual. He is a musician, poet, philosopher, fighter.

Meaning if inverted - Unbalanced emotions. Uncontrolled passion. Imbalance leading to downfall. An unethical victory. Ill-health. In spite of a desire for change, the journey is postponed.

In a reading - Conquest in business, emotions, or health. You will be successful. If his card is in the past, the person being read has had his success; the cards that follow indicate if it is a lasting one. They may also show the state of health. Reversed, there is a possibility of ill health.

Job and endeavors - The outcome is good. Battles won. Raise, promotion, acknowledgment. Loyalty is rewarded.

Meaning if reversed - Back-stabbing, delays, griping. Battles.

Romance and marriage - It is good, at least for the moment. The conquest is yours.

Resources - A turning point. It will be good. Outcome is positive. Just be sure to plan and stick to it. Reversed - could be car trouble. Loss. Not getting ahead.

Environment, path, and possibilities - Just do it. Less talk. More action.

Spiritual signpost Mankind has two natures which exist together, but are at times very opposed. Within us is an animal nature, and a nature that we like to think of as "human". Without the animal nature we would not compete so fiercely. We would not be driven to achieve, excel, explore, or conquer. The idea of "conquering" has allowed us to explore space, disease, oceans, and our own minds. It is what makes us passionate.

Without the other side of our nature, we would have no limits, love, or compassion. This side of our nature keeps us from being simple brutes.

The left rein and right rein must be held steady in order to stir the course between these two sides of what we are. To be a controlled, capable, strong, compassionate spirit, to have the strength of a man and the heart of a woman, this is to be human. See the movie "Ben Hur".

Pro 16:32 He that is slow to anger is better that the mighty; and he that ruleth his spirit than he that taketh a city.

Pro 17:3 The fining pot is for silver, and the furnace for gold: but the Lord trieth the Heart.

Strength - Card 8 of the Major Arcana

Meaning if upright - Inner love and inner peace, inner strength will triumph. Love is always stronger and lasts longer than hate. Quiet, focused determination. Patience is not passive, patience is concentrated strength. The balance of all sides of one's nature. Fear or hate released. When in the lion's den, Daniel overcame the lions with God's love and grace, not fear, hate, or aggression.

I will overcome pride by being humble. I will overcome hate with love. I will overcome selfishness with generosity ... And my restlessness with the peace of meditation.   Chinese proverb

Meaning if inverted - The material side dominates the spirit. . Fear, passion, or hate has you frozen. Discord within or without. The material or base drives at the expense of the mental and spiritual parts of the whole.

In a reading - Things are in motion by sheer will and determination instead of applying love This card shows that he has handled the situation well. Reversed, of course, it shows that things have been handled badly.

Job and endeavors - A hard job will be pulled off. Reversed - you may need help on a difficult assignment.

Romance and marriage - You may have an encounter with the wild side. Reversed - are trapped or obsessed by this relationship.

Resources - Cut back on luxuries. Stop with what you need, not what you want.

Environment, path, and possibilities - Cooperate. Give and take.

Meaning if reversed - You will be used if you don't take a stand.

Spiritual signpost Having reached the aim of the Chariot card naturally gives way to the condition of this card. Do not use outward force to subdue. Tyranny is always overthrown. Overlords are eventually lorded over, but a person who inspires confidence, admiration, and trust will be sought out even in his or her old age.

Daniel did not overcome the lions by fighting them. When he was dropped into the lion's den, he moved with peace and love, protected by the inner strength God gave him. The scriptures say that Daniel had an "excellent spirit" in him. Dan. 6:1 - 28

Gal 5:22 But the fruit of the spirit is love, joy, peace, longsuffering, gentleness, goodness, faith, meekness, temperance: against such there is no law.

1Cor 13:1 Though I speak with the tongues of men and of angels, and have not charity (agape'), I am become as sounding brass, or tinkling cymbal. And though I have the gift of prophecy, and understand all mysteries, and all knowledge; and though I have all faith, so that I could remove mountains, and have not charity, I am nothing.

The Hermit - Card 9 of the Major Arcana

Meaning if upright - Counsel; a meeting with one who will guide you. The courage, insight, and maturity to do what is right. Prudence. The willingness to accept help when offered. The search for inner peace and wisdom. If you want to know how to reach the mountain top, ask the man who lives there. When the student is ready the teacher appears.

Meaning if inverted - Shallowness. Wisdom. Rejection of wise advice. Down-playing one's own maturity. Foolish vices. Refusal to learn from mistakes or to experience new things.

In a reading - People are often pig-headed and refuse to accept any other way of doing things. If this card comes up in the past of the person being read, then he has been offered some wise advice; the following few cards will show whether he has been able to accept it or not. If the card is in the future, suggest to him that when unselfish help is offered he should not turn it down. If reversed and in the past, it indicates that the person being read has already refused some help from an older and wiser person; if reversed and in the future, suggest to him that instead of turning down the help that will be offered, he should give the matter further thought to see if the help is of real value to him. This card can also suggest that the person being read lives in a childish world of his own and refuses to grow up. If the person being read is a woman, she does not want to act or dress according to her own age, but like a much younger person.

Job and endeavors - Give and take advice. Exchange ideas.

Romance and marriage - Someone returns from a trip. Time away in order to fully examine and understand your feelings.

Resources - Invest in self-improvement and education. Seek advice before signing contracts

Environment, path, and possibilities - Back off and meditate. Think before you act.

Spiritual signpost - It is difficult to listen graciously to others at times. When they don't agree with our opinions, we often reject the advice without thought. Most viewpoints do have something to offer. There is something to learn from everyone if the mind is open.

Conversely, for most people, the question is not asked if the heart is not ready to hear the answer. Do offer advice when not asked. Keep your own counsel. It is as important to know when to speak than what to say.

The Hermit card represents the prophets of the Bible, those who were chosen because of a different way of viewing the world. These men did not see in the physical plane, but they looked into the spiritual nature of things.

II Ki 3:9 - 22 They saw possibilities through faith.

Pro 1:2 To know wisdom and instruction; to perceive the words of understanding; To receive the instruction of wisdom, justice, and equity; To give subtlety to the simple, to the young man knowledge and discretion. A wise man will hear, and will increase learning; and a man of understanding shall attain unto wise counsels:

The Wheel of Fortune – Card 10 of the Major Arcana

Meaning if upright - The winds of change. Fate brings success. The unexpected arrival of good fortune. New conditions. The cycle of life changes. The laws of chance are in your favor. Personal vision. A Jewish fable tells the story of King David who called his most talented craftsman and told him to make a ring for him. This ring was to have the power to stabilize the king's emotions. When he was overjoyed, it was to make him sober. When he was sad, it was to cheer him. The artisan went away perplexed and worried, having no idea how to fulfill the king's wish. On the way back to his home, he met the king's son, Solomon. Solomon, seeing the man was very worried, inquired as to his problem. The man explained. Solomon smiled and told the man how to accomplish his mission. Make a plain and unadorned ring, Solomon told him, and engrave on it these words..."THIS TOO SHALL PASS."

Meaning if inverted -A change for the worse. Bad luck. Set-backs. Courage and patience are the tools to get you by. This too will pass.

In a reading - An unusual turn of luck. Success. Fate smiles on you. If this card is near a King, Queen, or Knight, one of the people represented by these cards contributes to your fate. If The Wheel of Fortune is the last card in the spread, the final outcome of his question seems to be out of his hands. He must simply apply all his knowledge and strength to overcome the negative conditions. When reversed, set-backs, bad luck. A better future must be built by will power and endurance.

Job and endeavors - Change brings opportunity. Loans come through. Resources are up.

Romance and marriage - Go for it. Nothing is forever but this is worth a chance.

Resources - Things fluctuate. Job and endeavors; the market.

Environment, path, and possibilities - Before signing contracts prepare as best you can, then play the odds.

Spiritual signpost But if not for the grace of God, there go I. It is a function of time itself that changes things. Entropy is the rule of the universe. Things combine to breakdown and re-combine in various forms. It is difficult to accept change, especially if the change is not positive. The only assurance is that bad situations won't last... but then, neither will the good. Can we, like the Apostle Paul, let grace abound whether abased or exalted. Can you keep the faith when hell breaks loose around you? That is the test.

Job 14:14 If a man die, shall he live again? All the days of my appointed time will I wait, till my change come.

Job 14:19 The waters wear the stones: thou washest away the things which grow out of the dust of the earth; and thou destroyest the hope of man. Thou prevailest for ever against him...

Ecc 3:1 3 To every thing there is a season, and a time to every purpose under the heaven: 2 A time to be born, and a time to die; a time to plant, and a time to pluck up that which is planted;
3 A time to kill, and a time to heal; a time to break down, and a time to build up; 4 A time to weep, and a time to laugh; a time to mourn, and a time to dance; 5 A time to cast away stones, and a time to gather stones together; a time to embrace, and a time to refrain from embracing; 6 A time to get, and a time to lose; a time to keep, and a time to cast away; 7 A time to rend, and a time to sew; a time to keep silence, and a time to speak; 8 A time to love, and a time to hate; a time of war, and a time of peace.

Justice – Card 11 of the Major Arcana

Meaning if upright - Getting what is deserved, what ever that means. Justice will be done. Balance. Seeing all sides of a situation. Arbitration. Lawsuits will be won. A balanced personality demands elimination of preconceptions and prejudices. Cultivating the objective mind. A balance between business and home or between the material and spiritual. Do not confuse what is right with what you must do to survive. Do not confuse what is legal with what is right.

Meaning if inverted - Injustice, inequality. Legal complications. A biased mind. Subjective, illegal, deceitful, boorish, prejudice, excessive, severity.

In a reading - With this card, it could mean the person will win a lawsuit. Balanced judgment is also indicated. Informed choices. The outcome of a lawsuit, if one was pending, will be just to all. When reversed, the person has experienced injustice or the loss of a lawsuit. You would be wise not to go to court. Prejudiced, selfishness, clouded mind. If a Court Card is present, the meaning may apply to that person.

Job and endeavors - Tests are coming. Play by the book.

Romance and marriage – Be open, honest, and accepting.

Resources - Examine the pros and cons.

Environment, path, and possibilities - You will be held accountable. Don't cut corners.

Spiritual signpost - What is justice? Getting what we deserve? Then may God help us all! None of us would go without punishment. This card is man's soon to be doomed attempt to do the job that God has set aside for himself. The Godly concept of judgment has fallen to the fallacy of justice. Justice is a human concept, administered by men as defiled as those for whom they mete out punishment. Justice is given without regard to the heart, which cannot be known by another. Justice always falls short of serving its purpose. When asked about justice, the Bible says, It is better to have mercy than to demand sacrifice. We fight to get what we deserve, only if it is the positive reward.

Take no revenge. Exact no price. Do unto others as if they were you. Wait and watch. They will dig their own grave. Justice is getting what is deserved, usually brought about by his or her own hands. Negative actions engender resistance by others. Let grace and mercy be part of the response also.

Zec 7:9 Thus speaketh the Lord of hosts, saying, Execute true judgment, and shew mercy and compassion every man to his brother: And oppress not the widow, nor the fatherless, the stranger, nor the poor; and let none of you imagine evil against his brother in your Heart.

Hos 6:6 For I desire mercy, and not sacrifice...

The Hanged Man – Card 12 of the Major Arcana

Meaning if upright - Upon his crucifixion, Saint Peter, the apostle, asked to be fixed upside down on the cross, stating that he was unworthy to be crucified in the fashion of Christ. This is the card of "turning it over to God." It represents spiritual growth; surrender to a higher wisdom. A complete reversal of one's usual way of life because of a spiritual change. Dependence no longer on the self but on God.

It may seem to some as indecision, but we must wait on God to work things out for us. The ability to preach or prophesy. All of the 12 step programs, from Alcoholics Anonymous to Cocaine Anonymous, contain the acknowledgment of a higher power and surrender to that power.

Meaning if inverted - A preoccupation with self. Ignoring those in need. Absorption in the physical. Turning away from the spiritual. Impatience. Trying to do things in your time and way instead of God's. Resistance to spiritual teachings. False prophecy.

In a reading - This card means seeking more spiritual instruction. Psychic ability. Reversed, it means enjoyment in the physical with no time to feed the soul. Reversed, it means not guided by the wisdom of others nor trust in the higher power. Trusting only your wits.

Job and endeavors - It may be time to try something new.

Romance and marriage - Different types and ways in a relationship. You must make a choice. It is best to let go.

Resources - Resources are tight. Cut back.

Environment, path, and possibilities - Wait. Think and watch before deciding. Things will come to light.

Spiritual signpost - *Just as I am, though tossed about with many a conflict, many a doubt, fighting within and fears without, O Lamb of God, I come. I come.* Charlotte Elliott 1786-1871

For many of us, the hardest thing to do is to trust our higher source. When things are not going well, it is difficult to say, "The universe is unfolding as it should."

Rom 1:1 Paul, a servant of Jesus Christ, called to be an apostle, separated unto the gospel of God.

1 Cor 9:19 For though I be free from all men, yet have I made myself a servant unto all, that I might gain the more.

Mat. 20:27 And whosoever will be chief among you, let him be your servant. Even as the son of man came not to be ministered unto, but to minister, and to give his life a ransom for many.

Surrender is the first step to a spiritual life ... and the hardest.

Death – Card 13 of the Major Arcana

Meaning if upright - Transfiguration, change which demands release or dissolution of something held dear. Renewal, transformation. New ideas, new possibilities. Destruction of the old, followed by birth of the new. Metamorphosis. The death of something within, thus a type of awakening.

Meaning if inverted - Stagnation; tendency to inertia. Wanting to break free but something constrains you. Revolution. Overthrow. Disaster.

In a reading - Renewal. If a Court Card appears, the change will come through that person. With the Moon - a time of purging, change, difficulties.

Job and endeavors - Change, termination, shake up. Things change for the good.

Romance and marriage - Paths will diverge. Endings, goodbyes, relationships change for ever.

Resources - It is time to cash in and hold on. Call in any resources you've loaned and sit tight.

Environment, paths, and possibilities - Time to start over or set new goals. Prepare to start anew.

Spiritual signpost - The moment of surrender begins the death of the old ways, and a new beginning. Loss of the old ways gives birth to a new spiritual life. I have never seen a caterpillar struggle to live. They lay down their meager lives with only the vaguest idea that it is not the end. The caterpillar builds his own coffin and without reluctance, crawls in. For the gracious acceptance of his fate he is presented with a new live. This is not a card of mortal death. It is a card of change. Go with grace.

Phil 3:21 Who shall change our vile body, that it may be fashioned like unto his glorious body...

Mar 9:1 ...There be some of them that stand here, which shall not taste of death, till they have seen the kingdom of God come with power.

The Death card represents the death, burial, and resurrection of Jesus, and the potential within all of us to spiritually follow in his footsteps. Our old nature can die and our true, deeper nature will be born.

Temperance – Card 14 of the Major Arcana

Meaning if upright - The combining of ingredients to form a substance stronger or better than either, such as the tempering of steel. Adaptation, self-control, modification, coordination, job and home in harmony. Harmony with others. The use of successful combinations. Good management and good balance in life. Artistic creations. Alchemy.

Meaning if inverted - Bad combinations. Unable to work together. Bad management; unfortunate combinations; competing interests in business or personal affairs. Lack of good judgment. Temperament out of balance.

In a reading - The word "temperance" is defined as the bringing together of two opposite qualities. It is another way of saying balance or combination. In a reading, this card would indicate bringing things together in successful combinations, for example, a partnership, or even in successfully mixing people. The surrounding cards indicate what the combination will be. When Temperance is reversed, unsuccessful combinations, or the combinations may be evil, such as introducing two co-dependants or sociopaths.

Job and endeavors - New strategies, breakthroughs, and ideas.

Romance and marriage - There is a special chemistry and attraction.

Resources - Put your assets to the job and endeavors. Hobbies make good resources.

Environment, path, and possibilities - A good time to put all of the pieces together.

Spiritual signpost - A better name for this card would be "synergy." The reference here is not to the temperance movement, but to the tempering of steel. Synergy is the correct combination of two or more ingredients that yield more than its components. In the making of steel iron and carbon are combined in the correct fashion to yield a substance much harder and stronger than either of the components. When the ingredients of correct occupation, correct thought, correct action, correct speech, and correct hobby, are reached, the human soul is in balance and is set free. Anything is possible. The Temperance card is a picture of the potential available when the spirit of God is combined with any individual life. Retrace the path. First, spiritual surrender, then the death of the old ways, next, the spirit of God combines with us to lead us on.

1 Co 12:4 Now there are diversities of gifts, but the same Spirit.

1 Co 12:6 And there are diversities of operations, but it is the same God which worketh in all.

1 Co 12:8 For to one is given by the Spirit the word of wisdom; to another the word of knowledge by the same Spirit;

The Devil – Card 15 of the Major Arcana

Meaning if upright - The situation looks bad because you only see things from one side. Use a new viewpoint. Trapped by your old, worn habits or ways of thinking. Greed or fear hold you in a bad situation. Same mistake made again. Greed, fear, or ego eclipses the spirit. Temptation, illness, a perverse sexual desire. Disregard for human dignity. The inhumane or wrongful use of force. Bondage to the material; revolution; black magic; evil. Overthrow, savage sexuality. Oppression.

Meaning if inverted - You have learned a life lesson. You may never have to go through it again. You have removed the chains that held you. Overcoming pride and selfishness. Release. Black magic has no power over the person. Help comes from God. Other sources say this card can indicate a weak and timid person, ineffectual, and indecisive.

In a reading - Dependence on the material rather than the spiritual. As to evil influences; the cards next to it indicate whether he has overcome them. A Court Card would identify the sort of person who exerted this influence. One of the Aces would mean that a new beginning is possible. Temptation. The card following will show whether he will resist this temptation. No profit in wrongdoing. Reversed, this card means that evil influences have been resisted or overcome. The chains about the nude figures in the card are loose and can be removed by them at anytime. With the Magician - things are peculiar. Strange occurrences.

Job and endeavors - You are trapped in a bad situation. A company or boss is taking advantage of you. They act as if they own you. It is scary but it's time to get out.

Romance and marriage - Cruelty, abuse, or nagging. You feel trapped. A friend may be sick.

Resources - The more you make the more you spend. Job, money, and endeavors at a low point. Trapped.

Environment, path, and possibilities - Stand up for your rights. Deals go bad. Prepare.

Spiritual signpost - Want to know how to catch a monkey? Take a jar with an opening just big enough for a monkey's hand to fit into. Place something the monkey wants in the jar. Bury the jar with only the top showing. Monkeys are curious and greedy. It will seize the object of its delight and will refuse to let it go, even when the humans come and capture the monkey. They will have to dig the jar up and remove it with the monkey to its new prison home. The animal will not even entertain the thought of letting it go. Evolution hasn't accomplished all that much, has it?

Think new thoughts in new ways and the traps you face will become stepping stones. There is one comment regarding the Devil card. There is only one devil and he is in only one place at a time, therefore I can only assume we cause most of our trouble ourselves. Let's give the devil his due, and us, ours. It is easy to forget the grace that has brought us thus far and fall back into the pit from which we came. The Devil card represents eternal entropy that tends to pull us back into old ways and habits. We are beckoned back, not because the old ways are better, but because they are familiar. We must not forget that those ways never worked.

Luk 22:31 And the Lord said, Simon, Simon, behold, Satan hath desired to have you, that he may sift you as wheat: But I have prayed for thee, that thy fail not: and when thou art converted, strengthen thy brethren.

Mat 4:11 Then the devil leaveth him, and, behold, angels came and ministered unto him.

The Tower – Card 16 of the Major Arcana

Meaning if upright – Breakdown of a car or major appliance. Your selfishness and ego bring you down. Ambition is about to be brought low. Conflict, change, unforeseen catastrophe. Old notions upset. Chance of bankruptcy. Overthrow of a lifestyle. Disruption. A sudden or unexpected change that may temporarily upset your life.

Meaning if inverted - Same as before, but in lesser degree. Breakdowns. False accusations, gossip, loss, oppression.

In a reading - Breakdowns that are costly or unexpected. Success built on a shoddy foundation. Products or methods breakdown. Ambition runs away. A fall. You may face bankruptcy and ruin if continuing on the present course. Pride goeth before a fall, and the fall is coming. If found with Court Cards, it will signify the sort or person who may be responsible for the downfall. A spiritual card will show that he has learned his lesson. In the reversed position, this card means much the same thing to a lesser degree.
Failures, a less serious fall. A Court Card near the tower may mean someone is falsely accusing him of wrongdoing. The Tower can indicate a negative outcome as the 10th card of a Celtic Cross spread. It indicates that in spite of best efforts, not everything goes as planned.

Job and endeavors - Things go bad or break. Scandals.

Romance and marriage - Lies, infidelity, no trust, feelings of abandonment.

Resources - Resources misapplied. Guard against loss, theft, fire.

Environment, path, and possibilities - Act fast or you'll lose. Situation turns bad.

Spiritual signposts - There is little comfort in this card for the immediate future. If we succumb to these types of cards, this is where we end. It is a sign of disorder, destruction, and chaos. Yet, when buildings are torn down, we can rebuild in the fashion we choose. This is the falling away and destruction of the present. The future is in your hands. Try to remember that spiritual growth is accelerated in times of physical hardship, if you can endure and see past the present discomfort. This card is the lesson of hard knocks. Lessons revisited the hard way may be learned finally.

1 Th 5:2 For yourselves know perfectly that the day of the Lord so cometh as a thief in the night. 1 Th 5:3 For when they shall say, Peace and Safety; then sudden destruction cometh upon them...

Pro 16:18 Pride goeth before destruction, and a haughty spirit before a fail.

The Tower card is symbolic of the Tower of Babel, where the haughty presumption of mankind led to the attempt to reach heaven itself. The sin of the attempt was not that man tried to reach toward God, but rather the urge to make gods of men. In lieu of improving their spiritual lives and drawing nigh to God, the builders turned to physical substitutes, and fell. The higher we climb, the further we fall. Ascension will happen of its own accord.

The Star – Card 17 of the Major Arcana

Meaning if upright - Courage, hope, inspiration. Gifts of the spirit. Good health. Help comes with no strings attached. Great romance and marriage possible. Insight into the meanings of life. A new and better situation. A temporary calm. Finding your center.

Meaning if inverted - Doubt, pessimism, stubbornness. Blind to your own faults. Lack of objectivity. Loss of friendship, romance, or marriage. Chance of illness. Delusion.

In a reading - You will experience good things. The cards surrounding will indicate what is in store. Health will improve; there will be new friendships or the old ones will deepen. A romance or marriage will lead to happiness. In business or profession good things will happen. Contacts or associates are very helpful. You must follow you heart. Reversed, in either the past or future means caution must be used. Health must watched. Pessimism and doubt may cause something resembling nervousness or depression.

Job and endeavors - Untangle, concentrate. Focus on your priority and you'll make it.

Romance and marriage - Time to cultivate that relationship.

Resources - Lots of cash flows through with little saved. Manage better.

Environment, path, and possibilities - Focus on one thing at a time. Don't spread yourself too thin.

Spiritual signpost - Hope is the beginning of all great things. Hope is the fuel that powers the doing. Hope, after having fallen, allows us to get up and try again. The righteous man, the scriptures declare, if he falls seventy times will get up and try again.

Rom 4:18 Who against hope believed in hope, that he might become the father of many nations...

1 Co 13:13 And now abideth faith, hope, and charity, these three, but the greatest of these is charity

Gal 5:5 For we through the Spirit wait for hope of righteousness by faith.

The Moon – Card 18 of the Major Arcana

Meaning if upright - Peril, deception, change. Bad luck for yourself or someone you know. Intuition, dreams, psychic powers. Unseen danger. Emotions are frayed. Apprehension. Urges you do not understand drive you.

Meaning if inverted - Change, imagination, deception will be unmasked. Major misunderstandings. No risks should be taken. Do not gamble. Watch for being set up by someone.

In a reading - Going through perils not foreseen. Perhaps he is a developing psychic or intuit. Watch for misfortune to yourself or someone close to you. In reverse, the moon is not really a bad card, since it cancels out things that are suggested when right side up. It is of great importance if it represents the person being read, because it may mean the development of psychic gifts.

Job and endeavors - Pace yourself. Be careful if you are sneaking around.

Romance and marriage - Party time. Running with the wolves. Anything goes.

Resources - Very unstable.

Environment, path, and possibilities - Go with your instincts.

Spiritual signpost - Logic has its limits. It is only half of our true nature. It is time to rely on your feelings about people and events. Trust yourself. There are hidden meanings, hidden agendas, and hidden truths. Only your intuition can show you the right way.

The Moon card is unconscious urges and lunacy, guided intuition or madness. It represents things hidden within or without. It is not only our own nature that we fight, but the nature of others. Whether it be that misery loves company, or that affirmation is found in others, in general people wish us to be like them. They will pull us back into the mire they have not yet escaped, if we let them.

Pro 25:18 A man that beareth false witness against his neighbor is a maul, and a sword, and a sharp arrow.
IKi 22:23 Now therefore behold, the Lord hath put a lying spirit in the mouth of these thy prophets, and the Lord hath spoken evil concerning thee.

Psa 31:13 For I have heard the slander of many: fear was on every side: while they took counsel together against me, they devised to take away my life. But I trusted in thee, O Lord: I said, Thou art my God.

The Sun – Card 19 of the Major Arcana

Meaning if upright - This is one of the best cards. Success, attainment; a good relationship develops. Achievements, birth. Studies completed. Learning that brings promotion. Happiness, pleasure in life. Good health. Victory, creativity.

Meaning if inverted - Plans clouded. Setbacks. Trouble in an important relationship. A broken engagement. Failure. Loss of a valued object.

In the reading - Look at the cards around it to find what kind of success and happiness will come to the person. It can mean a good relationship. A happy marriage. Success in business. If the sun comes after a "bad" card, the matter will be cleared up. If the Sun comes before a bad card it means you can overcome or avoid the problem. With the Moon - memory, experience, struggle.

Job and endeavors - Break free. Do things differently. New ways and thoughts bring success.

Romance and marriage - Let things run their course. Let it boil.

Resources - Buy, spend, fix up, buy clothes, throw a party. Splurge.

Environment, path, and possibilities - Move with the spirit. Life is not a march, it is a dance.

Spiritual signpost - After the dark night of the soul, the spiritual sun rises. With love, mercy, compassion, and intuition awakened, we integrate them into our psyche. We are now birthed as a complete person.

The progression of rebirth can be seen in the progression through the Devil card, Death card, Judgment card, and the Sun card. At first we resist our destiny, holding on to our lower conscience out of fear and ignorance. When we finally realize that we are so limited and trapped in our state, we give up and let go. The old dies and is changed according to its faith into a new creature. This is the dawning and the awakening of our soul's new life. The Sun rises within us for the first time.

Joh 3:3 ...Except a man be born of water and spirit, he can not enter the kingdom of God. That which is born of flesh is flesh; and that which is born of the Spirit is spirit.

1 Pe 1:23 Being born again, not of corruptible seed, but of incorruptible, by the word of God, which liveth and abideth for ever.

Judgment – Card 20 of the Major Arcana

Meaning if upright - A spiritual resurrection. Awakening; renewal. A good life. Job and endeavors well done. Universal consciousness glimpsed. The universal. Spiritual awakening. Renewed energy, better health, a quicker mind. Out of the ashes, the phoenix rises. You are stronger for having learned a lesson.

Meaning if inverted - The fear of death or failure keeps you from seeing clearly. Failure in finding happiness. No interest in the spiritual side of environment. Possible loss, ill health.

In a reading - If it appears in the future, a spiritual awakening is to come. If it is in the past, the person has already had an awakening of some sort, and the rest of the cards will indicate whether he has followed this up or let it dry up or fade away. In reverse, Judgment indicates a type of failure to find spiritual or material niche. As the last card in a spread, Judgment would mean a good ending, and suggests a spiritual lesson will be learned. With the Strength card - a strong and good decision. With Justice and Hanged Man - trials will help you clarify your purpose.

Job and endeavors - Things become very clear.

Romance and marriage - A past romance or marriage re-enters. A good experience.

Resources - A wind-fall. Resources come and troubles end.

Environment, path, and possibilities - Things turn. Endings. The outcome is good.

Spiritual signpost - As the Sun card represents our birth and fledgling steps as an integrated and complete persona, Judgment is the card of a person functioning with his expanded consciousness.

You must continue to allow yourself to be guided by your inner sense. The Judgment card depicts the resurrection of the saints as described in I Thes. 4:13 -18.

In the Tarot, this is a metaphor of an awakened spirit within us. The sleeper must awake!

Dan 12:12 And many of them that sleep in the dust of the Earth shall awake, some to everlasting life, and some to shame and everlasting contempt.

Joh 11:11 ...Our friend Lazarus sleepeth, but I go, that I may awake him out of sleep.

Eph 5:14 Wherefore he saith, Awake thou that sleepest, and arise from the dead, and Christ shall give thee light.

The World – Card 21 of the Major Arcana

Meaning if upright - This is the best card in the deck and is the good conclusion of matters. Fulfillment. Desires satisfied. Reward, success. Move ahead in all undertakings. The ability to make others happy. Change of residence or job. Travel. Intuition and psychic insights. The path of liberation. Victory. Correct combination of life elements.

Meaning if inverted - Goals postponed. Success to be won. Fear of change. Lack of insight or vision. Refusal to learn the lessons shown in the other cards.

In a reading - This can be called the best card in the deck. When it appears in a seeker's lay out, the material and spiritual outcome is good. If it is inverted, things will not be to your satisfaction. As the final card in a spread, it can be terrific. The most important use of the Tarot must be to make us think and reflect on our spiritual evolution. With the 5 of Cups, emotional disappointment.

Job and endeavors - Things won't be clear for one year. This is a new beginning but an unclear choice.

Romance and marriage - New romance and marriage. The real thing.

Resources - Time to start a new system.

Environment, path, and possibilities - A time of change and waiting to see.

Spiritual signpost – After years of study, research, and agony, I finally reached my academic goal and received my advanced degree; as he shook my hand, my counselor said to me, "Congratulations, you have made it to the starting line. Now the real growth and learning begins."

This card is taken from the attained goal of heaven. It is the end of the journey and the reward for which we have endured such pain. Growth is not easy. It always comes with a price. We lose friends, ways of life, and even the idea of our self. It all must be counted as lost as soon as the journey begins. In the Biblical sense, this card should be renamed Heaven. And, make no mistake; we must go through hell to get there.

Mat 6:33 But seek ye first the kingdom of God, and his righteousness; and all these things shall be added unto you.

Mat 17:2 And (he) was transfigured before them: and his face did shine as the sun, and his raiment was white as the light.

The Fool – Card 0 of the Major Arcana

Meaning if upright - The Fool represents the beginning of all creativity and the desire to accomplish selfless or selfish goals. Here are all possibilities both good and bad. Choices and cross roads. A new choice is before you. Be careful and choose wisely. Innocence or foolishness. Childishness or childlike. Spontaneity or childishness may lead to choices and actions not logical or well thought out.

Meaning if inverted - The choice is likely to be faulty and lead to thoughtless action. Fear may hold you back. Childishness is warned against.

In the reading - When this card appears in the future of the person being read, it represents a future choice. The fool card represents a fork in the road. The decision before you is one of "left or right" and many times there is no map to guide you. Act with the knowledge and wisdom of others who have traveled the path. If there are many Major Arcana in the spread, then the person being read does not have much to say about it because the decisions or choices will be made by others or by the situation itself.

When the Fool is found in reverse, warn the person being read that his choice is foolish, selfish or childish. When it is in the past, the person being read has already made a choice of some importance, and the cards surrounding it will tell whether the choice was a good one. With the Death card or Wheel of Fortune, change is bound to happen. With the 9 or 10 of Swords, change will bring negative results. With the 8 of Swords you will want to change but will feel tied down.

Job and endeavors - Change. New job or new path and possibilities in your present job. You will desire a fresh start. Just make sure it is a wise choice. With an Ace of Pentacles a new job is probable. With the 8 or 3 of Pentacles the job and endeavors will work out well. With the 4 or 5 of Pentacles the change is not recommended. With the 5 of

Wands there is an unsure conflict. With the 7 of Wands you will have a struggle but also the upper hand.

Romance and marriage - Seeking a new partner or friend. Thinking about an affair. With the Ace of Cups a new relationship is near or has just started. With the 2 of Cups a friendship is likely. With the 3 of Cups it is likely to be more than friends and you will also be sexually drawn to them. With the 4 of Wands there will be harmony. With the 5 of Wands there will be contention. With the 3 of Swords, romance and marriage will be in disarray.

Resources - Don't splurge. Be careful. New opportunities are here. With the 6 of Pentacles things will be profitable. With the 7 of Pentacles you will wait longer than you want.

Environment, path, and possibilities - A leap of faith is called for. If you don't have the faith, then don't leap. With any Ace, go for it. With the World or the Sun, go for it. With the Tower you should hold your position for a time.

Spiritual signpost - A child has no rules and sees no restriction, but has no wisdom. You must keep the first and guard against the second. The difference between the two is the latter has all knowledge and knows no restrictions.

Mat 18:3 ... Except ye be converted and become as little children, ye shall not enter the kingdom of heaven.

Mat 18:4 Whosoever shall humble himself as this little child, the same is greatest in the kingdom of heaven.

The Fool represents Christ himself. The Fool, being numbered "0", or having no number at all, is the beginning and ending of all spiritual qualities represented within the deck. Just as God is the Alpha and Omega, the beginning and the end of all things; Christ is both maker and judge of all. Christ, whose name was Jesus, became a fool for our account. He was rejected by the religious authorities and shunned by most of mankind because of one simple fact. He became as a child, doing only what his father in heaven told him. He was free of the world's rules. He had no preconceived ideas as to his limits. He knew no bonds, thus anything his Father in heaven told him to do, he did. We should be so humble. We should be so unlimited. We should be so powerful. We should all aspire to be the image of Christ.

1CO 1:19-23 For it is written, I will destroy the wisdom of the wise, and will bring to nothing the understanding of the prudent. Where is the wise? Where is the scribe? Where is the disputer of this world? Hath not God made foolish the wisdom of this world? For after that in the wisdom of God the world by wisdom knew not God, it pleased God by the foolishness of preaching to save them that believe. For the Jews require a sign, and the Greeks seek after wisdom: But we preach Christ crucified, unto the Jews a stumbling block, and unto the Greeks foolishness.

MINOR ARCANA

The Minor Arcana represents the more mundane events in life. Most of our day to day activities can be summed up in the Minor Arcana. The fifty-six cards of the Minor Arcana are divided into four categories or suits. They are Swords, Wands, Pentacles, and Cups.

For the most part, the Minor Arcana deals with balancing and harmonizing life situations, events, and feelings. Everyday problems such as loss or gain, satisfaction or dissatisfaction, leaving or staying, fighting or peace, reward or tyranny, love or discord, anxiety or joy, creativity or destruction, are all represented in the symbols and pictures of these cards.

The four suits represent certain things:

Wands

Also known as staffs, spears, rods.
Element: FIRE
The "budding" of the Ace of Wands reminds me of the budding trees of Springtime. In the Tree of Life.
Passion, ambition, career, creative endeavors, religion, philosophy. Acting on a passion to accomplish. Adventure, invention, inspirational. A speaker with zeal. Excitement and impatience, pursuits, grand ideals and gestures, and the desire to make one's

mark on the world. Temper, passion, desires, enthusiasm, charisma, competitiveness, athletics, and restlessness, travel and movement.

Cups

Also known as chalices, bowls, cauldrons.

Element: WATER

Summer – Cups represents the emotions. Cups are about romantic or poetic emotions, the heart. Sorrow, bliss, nostalgia, melancholy. Feelings toward one another. Emotional connection. Family or friends, sympathy or regret. Loneliness, loss. Emotional extremes such as elation or depression. Poetry, art, music or dance. Psychic powers, visions, illusions. The esoteric.

Swords

Also known as knives, daggers, blades.

Element: AIR.

Winter - Swords represent the mind and the voice. Here is the suit of sharp ideas and sharp tongues, of thinking things through or thinking/saying too much. Swords are cleverness and a love of facts, solving problems, performing calculations, discussing and debating. The suit is also, however, about braggarts and gossips, liars and slanderers. Anxiety, worry, problems and troubles. Writing, research, television, radio and the internet. Information and so the card of science, mathematics and medicine as well as debate, analysis and journalism.

Pentacles

Also known as disks or coins.

Element: EARTH

Autumn – Harvest and reflection, as well as preserving the bounty of the summer. Autumn is often a busy and materialistic time of year.

Health, money, luck and work. Physical work. Body, home, valuables. Solid matter, the real and physical world. Pragmatic, common sense, job/work. Possessions, money, bills. Indulging, luxuries, things that money can buy. One step at a time, slow-growth, long-term, building things. Bankers, accountant, business owners, craftsmen, farmers, shopkeepers and laborers, baker. Greed vs. generosity, luck and wealth.

The subsequent pages give the meaning for each of the Minor Arcana. The explanations are in two paragraphs, meaning if upright, and meaning if inverted (or up side down). If there are any combinations of cards that have special significance, they will also be mentioned. Lastly, there is a quote from the Bible. This quote is tied to the card in a general way and will further open the meaning of the card. Unlike the Major Arcana, the Minor Arcana does not connect directly with a spiritual path nor is it directly related to Scriptures. Instead, the Scriptures, being all encompassing, have been researched to give insight into the meaning of each numbered card. The Court

Cards do not have any Scripture attached to them since they represent personality traits and not life situations.

SWORDS

Swords

Representing aggression, assertiveness, turmoil.

Ace of Swords

Meaning if upright - Beginning of conquest. Birth of a strong willed child. Ideas, invention, creations, initiative, drive. Dawning of something good. Emotions with power. Beginnings of romance or marriage. Victory.

Meaning if inverted - Obstacles, tyranny, attempting to win by strong arming. Trying to overpower to gain your ends. Being caught in your own trap. Hate or revenge sought.

Psalms 18:32 It is God that girdeth me with strength, and maketh my way perfect. 18:35 He teacheth my hands to war so that a bow of steel is broken by my arms. 1 Ti 6:15 ...

2 of Swords

Meaning if upright - There is a need for balanced emotions. A stalemate. Indecision. Possible trouble ahead. A temporary truce but guarded and stiff. The person being read has a sense of balance and rhythm, but is in need of direction or opportunity. A feeling of being split, bound, or trapped by the situation. A two edged sword. Caught between Scylla and Charybdis.

Meaning if inverted - Release, movement in one's affairs, but with a warning regarding choices of the wrong path. Don't trust without first trying.

With the 2 of Pentacles - watch, wait, things are changing.

Ecc. 10:6 Folly is set in great dignity, and the rich sit in low places.
10:7 1 have seen servants upon horses and princes walking as servants upon the Earth.

Psalm 46:10 Be still, and know that I am God: I will be exalted among the heathen, I will be exalted in the earth.

3 of Swords

Meaning if upright - Stormy weather for the affections. A separation, quarrels, stress in relationships. An affair Is possible. Misfortune. Upheaval in the family or with a lover. Heartache, emotional discontent. Betrayal by a loved one.

Meaning if inverted - Disorder, confusion, loss. In a reading, the cards near the 3 of Swords will indicate the degree of sorrow, or from where it comes.

With the 5 of Swords - Fights or partial loss in romance and marriage.

Prov. 21:9 It is better to dwell in a corner of the housetop, than with a brawling woman in a wide house.

Prov. 18:1 through desire a man having separated himself, seeketh and intermeddleth with all wisdom.

4 of Swords

Meaning if upright - Being taken out of commission. Accident, illness, or loss of job will way-lay you. This condition is temporary and any illness will be minor. Rest and healing after strife or weakness. For the person being read it could mean a time of retreat, a sense of banishment or exile. There will soon be a change back to the active environment. Regroup.

Meaning if inverted - Renewed activity. Recovery. Renewed health. Caution not to trust everyone.

With 10 of Swords – sickness, layoff; With 9 of Swords - sickness

I Kings 17:2 And the word of the Lord came unto him, saying, Get thee hence, and turn thee eastward, and hide thyself by the brook...

Luke 22:41 And he was withdrawn from them about a stone's cast and kneeled down, and prayed...

5 of Swords

Meaning if upright - What does it gain you to win and trade a piece of your conscience for the prize? It is an empty victory. Failure, defeat, cruelty, or conquest by manipulation or unfair means. Theft. Trouble coming, temporary defeat. Picking a fight, taunting.

Meaning if inverted - There is still a chance of loss or defeat, but in lesser degree. An empty or unfair victory. manipulation, extortion.

Mat. 27:3 Then Judas which had betrayed him (Jesus), when he saw that he was condemned, repented himself, and brought again the thirty pieces of silver to the chief priests and elders.

6 of Swords

Meaning if upright - A journey that could be by or over water. Transcending difficulties or sorrow. Harmony. Emissaries are sent. A raising of awareness or conscience. Something triggers you to break free and make a change.

Meaning if inverted - Way out of present difficulties is slow in coming. A planned trip is postponed. You are stalled in your evolution, committing the same mistakes again. With the 6 of Wands - a major breakthrough.

Acts 8:39 And when they were come up out of the water, the spirit of the Lord caught away Philip... But Philip was found at Azotus.

Psa. 107:23 They that go down to the sea in ships, that do business in great waters; these see the works of the Lord, and his wonder in the deep.

Acts 13:4 So they, being sent forth by the Holy Ghost, departed unto Seleucia; and from thence they sailed to Cyprus.

7 of Swords

Meaning if upright - You have taken on too much, this makes you unreliable. You have promised more than you can easily deliver. Betrayal of confidence, spying. A plan that may fail. Flight from consequences of an act. Theft. Trying to make off with what is not yours. Other sources say, design, hope, an attempt, a plan made.

Meaning if inverted - Overqualified. You may be shooting too low. Good advice given. Recovery of stolen goods.

Acts 5:3 But Peter said, Ananias, why hath Satan filled thine Heart to lie to the Holy Ghost, and to keep back part of the price of the land.

Lev. 19:11 Ye shall not steal, neither deal falsely, neither lie one to another.

With the King of Cups - a new business venture. With the Love card - romance and marriage when and where it counts.

8 of Swords

Meaning if upright - Fearful of making a choice. A feeling of entrapment, bondage or restriction. Indecision. You feel too restrained or tightly held. Helplessness. Dissatisfaction. Censure. Temporary illness or sabotage.

Meaning if inverted - Overcoming fear. New beginnings now possible. Freedom from restrictions, release. With the 2 of Swords - feeling tied and bound in a situation. Can't shake loose.

Dan. 3:25 Did we not cast three men bound into the midst of the fire?... Lo, I see four men loose, walking in the midst of the fire, and they have no hurt; and the form of the fourth is like the Son of God.

ROM 8:14 For as many as are led by the Spirit of God, they are the sons of God. For ye have not received the spirit of bondage again to fear; but ye have received the Spirit of adoption, whereby we cry, Abba, Father. The Spirit itself beareth witness with our spirit, that we are the children of God: And if children, then heirs; heirs of God, and joint-heirs with Christ.

9 of Swords

Meaning if upright - Suffering, doubt, suspicion. Anxiety, bad dreams. A chance of illness, or injury. A romance or marriage is under stress. Cruelty, loss, misery, unfounded lies. Grief, depression. Knowing something that you don't want to face. Emotional repression.

Meaning if inverted - Time brings healing. Patience, unselfishness, faithfulness are to be cultivated. Good news regarding a romance. With Strength card - painful lessons.

Job 7:13 - 14 When I say, My bed shall comfort me, my couch shall ease my complaint; then thou scarest me with dreams, and terrifiest me with visions:

Proverbs 3:24 When thou liest down, thou shalt not be afraid: yea, thou shalt lie down, and thy sleep shall be sweet.

Psalm 91:5 Thou shalt not be afraid for the terror by night; nor for the arrow that flieth by day;

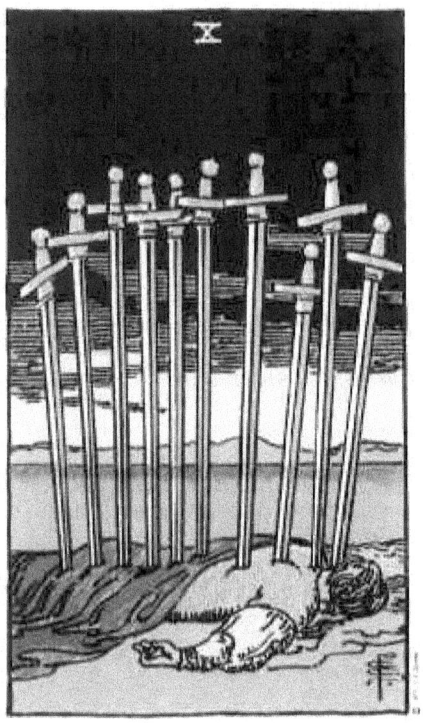

10 of Swords

Meaning if upright - Betrayal, deceit, a stab in the back. Treachery. Sudden misfortune; ruin of plans. Defeat. A legal battle lost. Failure, tears. Someone turns on you. Possible foul play.

Meaning if inverted - Courage to rise again. If a righteous man falls 70 times, he gets back up. Some success. Better health. Turning continuing problems over to God. With the Tower card - catastrophe, sickness, death. Loss

With the 3 of Swords - hurt by someone you care about.

Psa.37:14 The wicked have drawn out the sword, and have bent their bow, to cast down the poor and needy... Their sword shall enter into their own Heart and their bow shall be broken.

Psalm 56:1 Be merciful unto me, O God: for man would swallow me up; he fighting daily oppresseth me. 2 Mine enemies would daily swallow me up: for they be many that fight against me, O thou most High. 3 What time I am afraid, I will trust in thee.

Page of Swords

Meaning if upright - The qualities of dexterity, athletics, and diplomacy. Certain types of spying. An upsetting or abruptly delivered message.

Meaning if inverted - A tendency toward manipulation, or frivolity. An Impostor is likely to be exposed. Possibility of ill health. Abrupt change possible.

Knight of Swords

Meaning if upright - Someone is about to rush headlong into your life. A brave, domineering, courageous, skillful person. Could also mean the unexpected coming or going of a matter. Haste. Speaking or acting before you think.

Meaning if inverted - Tyranny over the helpless, be it man or animal. Always ready to start a fight. A troublemaker and brute. Sneaky, unfaithful one who can not be trusted

Queen of Swords

Meaning if upright - A woman who is perceptive, quick-witted, and confident. A woman of strong, even mannish nature. The spirit penetrates matter and yields intuition. Sternness. Someone beckons. Seeking balance or the reason behind things.

Meaning if inverted - Her powers or observations may lead her to be cruel. She has no tact. Sly or deceitful. Narrow-mindedness and tendency to gossip. With braided intent and braying tongue she drives him on like an ox goaded to the last inch of submission unaware that a man in love and at peace will lay down his sweat and life for love only. She drives him on, and away.

King of Swords

Meaning if upright - He is a judge, or judgmental. His is the commander, or wants to be. He is an authority figure. He is firm and over-cautious and suspicious. If his trust is won, he may be a wise counselor. Closed mindedness. Preparing to weather the storm. Set your mind and jaw for the coming situation. The battle joined.

Meaning if inverted - He is obstinate, malicious, judgmental, or cruel. Lawsuit could be lost. Arguments with those in authority do not seem fair.

PENTACLES

Pentacles
Representing business, resources, things owned, lost, or longed for

Ace of Pentacles

Meaning if upright - Attainment of a long term goal. Journey's end and, therefore, a new beginning. Beginnings of prosperity or business ventures. New starts, new beginnings. Happiness, pleasure. New ideas in finances. A new direction that brings better things. Things started should last. Starting a project that should do well. Material or financial gain. Determination, creativeness.

Meaning if inverted - Greed. Lack of initiative or tenacity. Plans fail. A good opportunity missed.

With 7 of Pentacles - a need to slow down and let things develop. With the Fool - things are coming out of nowhere.

Psa.50:10 For every beast of the forest is mine, and the cattle of a thousand hills. (God is rich, and if we are in accord with his will our share is accessible to us.)

2 of Pentacles

Meaning if upright - The ability to handle several situations at a time. Also able to maintain harmony in the midst of change. New projects may be difficult to launch due to details. Try to keep the big picture in mind. You may need to detach in order to maintain a balanced view. Attempting to balance a stressful situation.

Meaning if inverted - Difficulty in handling problems. He has too many irons in the fire. A discouraging message is likely to put a damper on his ideas. Obstacles, agitation, trouble, worry, nervousness. Details consume you.

With the 3 of Pentacles - business travel is likely. With the Judgment card - things may appear at a stand still but major decisions are about to be made.

Philippians 4:6 Be careful for nothing; but in every thing by prayer and supplication with thanksgiving let your requests be made known unto God. 7 And the peace of God, which passeth all understanding, shall keep your hearts and minds through Christ Jesus.

Colossians 2:1-23 ESV
For I want you to know how great a struggle I have for you and for those at Laodicea and for all who have not seen me face to face, that their hearts may be encouraged, being knit together in love, to reach all the riches of full assurance of understanding and the knowledge of God's mystery, which is Christ, in whom are hidden all the treasures of wisdom and knowledge. I say this in order that no one may delude you with plausible arguments. For though I am absent in body, yet I am with you in spirit, rejoicing to see your good order and the firmness of your faith in Christ. ...

3 of Pentacles

Meaning if upright - Skill, craftsmanship, ability. Work rewarded. Congratulations are due soon. Material success through ability and hard work. Construction, acknowledgment. Repair, rebuild.

Meaning if inverted - Mediocrity in job and endeavors. The person doesn't care enough. Things are delayed. Preoccupation with details and resources at the expense of the job. Common-place ideals and ambitions.

With the 9 of Pentacles - your skills are recognized.

Exo. 25:9 According to all that I shew thee, after the pattern of the tabernacle, and the pattern of all the instruments thereof, even so shall ye make it.

4 of Pentacles

Meaning if upright - Power, wealth, greed. Miserly, stingy, ungenerous. Too much worry over money whether it is in short supply or not. This person tends to live as if it is. Concentrated on getting and never giving. Financial stress has you locked up. Lack of charity has steeled your heart. Lonely. Keeping yourself distanced from others.

Meaning if inverted - Chance of loss. There will be obstacles, delay, and opposition to plans. A warning not to be too free with resources. Reversal of fortune.

I Ti. 6:10 For the love of money is the root of all evil: which while some coveted after, they have erred from the faith, and pierced themselves through with many sorrows.

5 of Pentacles

Meaning if upright – Poverty. Destitution in terms of money or love causes the human spirit to perish. Amidst the pressure of failure in life's challenges, there is a list. Do I have food, shelter, security, love? If any answer is no, our spirit starts to die. This card represents a temporary situation. Possibility of poor health, which should be watched. Spiritual impoverishment leads to despair. Dark night of the soul. Intense strain and extended stasis. Loss of employment.

Ruled by the heart. Romance and marriage or mistress. Disgraceful romance and marriage. Affairs. A person who is brilliant but not responsible.

Meaning if inverted - A lesson in charity is to be learned. New employment, but this may not be permanent. Revived courage. A new interest in spiritual matters.

With the Sun card- a more spiritual and charitable environment is coming. Destitute and dying of starvation, a widow and her son welcome a prophet into their hovel of a home. The prophet asks for something to eat. The widow uses the last of her meal.

IKing 17:14 Thus saith the Lord of Israel, the barrel of meal shall not waste, neither shall the cruse of oil fail, until the day of the Lord sendeth rain upon the earth.

Philippians 4:11 Not that I speak in respect of want: for I have learned, in whatsoever state I am, therewith to be content.
12 I know both how to be abased, and I know how to abound: every where and in all things I am instructed both to be full and to be hungry, both to abound and to suffer need.

6 of Pentacles

Meaning if upright - Present prosperity shared with others. Receiving what is rightfully yours. Philanthropy, charity, gifts. Tithing, donations. Success, prosperity. Small business dealings do well. Inheritance, unexpected money. Reward for efforts.

Meaning if inverted - A bribe. Unfairness in business or inheritance. Present prosperity threatened. Jealousy, greed, debts, extortion.

Acts 20:35 I have shewed you all things, how that so laboring ye ought to support the weak, and to remember the words of the Lord Jesus, how he said, it is more blessed to give than to receive.

Luke 6:38 Give, and it shall be given unto you; good measure, pressed down, and shaken together, and running over, shall men give into your bosom. For with the same measure that ye mete withal it shall be measured to you again.

7 of Pentacles

Meaning if upright - Growth through effort and initiative. This card represents the time between planting and harvest. A loan, an exchange, or sale. What has been planted will mature. The artist reevaluates his job and endeavors. Success; delay but ending in growth. Hard work. The beginning of a new enterprise.

Other viewpoints include - A stage of monetary stagnation. Blight, worry, melancholy, anxiety. A person in control will oppose you. Greed, wealth.

Meaning if inverted - Little gain after much work. Impatience, anxiety about a business deal. Unprofitable investments. Failure. Lack of hope.

With the 8 of Pentacles - immersing yourself in a project. Art.

Lev. 26:4 Then I will give you rain in due season, and the land shall yield her increase...

8 of Pentacles

Meaning if upright - Learning a trade, craft or profession. Apprenticeship. Training, schooling. Employment to come. Skill in job, hobbies, or art. Gain of resources. Craftsmanship, ambition. Religious or philosophic venture. Pride in your work.

Meaning if inverted - Wrong use of skills. Dislike of hard work. Easily bored. False vanity, voided ambition. Weighted down by details. Hypocrisy, waste, loss.

With the 3 of Cups - your ability and enterprise wins through.

2Ch. 4:11 And Huram made the pots, and the shovels, and the basins. And Huram finished the work that he was to do for King Solomon for the house of God.

Exodus 35:35 Them hath he filled with wisdom of heart, to work all manner of work, of the engraver, and of the cunning workman, and of the embroiderer, in blue, and in purple, in scarlet, and in fine linen, and of the weaver, even of them that do any work, and of those that devise cunning work.

9 of Pentacles

Meaning if upright - Material security. Refinement, class. Solitary enjoyment of the good things in life. Wisdom where one's own interests lie. Garden, home. Caution to be prudent. Inheritance. Increase. Loss of home or friend. The answer to the Question is a strong yes if other surrounding card verify this. Enjoyment of the harvest.

Meaning if inverted - Possible loss. Friendship, romance, home threatened. Thievery. Beware of legal troubles. Contracts and agreements may be broken. Move with caution. Deceit.

With the 3 and 6 of Pentacles - paid for job and endeavors completed. Overdue resources arrive.

With the 8 of Pentacles and the Magician - you will master this situation.

Eph. 1:8 Wherein he (God) hath abounded toward us in all wisdom and prudence.

2 Corinthians 9:8 And God is able to make all grace abound toward you; that ye, always having all sufficiency in all things, may abound to every good work:

10 of Pentacles

Meaning if upright - Family matters stabilized. Gain in wealth. Property is bought or inherited. Finances improve. Inheritance. Success, agreement, prosperity, gift, pension. Music, art, painting. Parents, kids, and grandparents get together. Contentment, wealth.

Meaning if inverted - Chance of family misfortune or loss. Remember, family usually does not work well together. This is not a good time to take risks. A problem concerning an agreement or contract. Watch it, you are not thinking clearly. Robbery, loss.

Pro. 31:23 Her husband is known in the gates, when he sitteth among the elders of the land.

Proverbs 3: 6 In all thy ways acknowledge him, and he shall direct thy paths. 7 Be not wise in thine own eyes: fear the Lord, and depart from evil. 8 It shall be health to thy navel, and marrow to thy bones. 9 Honour the Lord with thy substance, and with the firstfruits of all thine increase: 10 So shall thy barns be filled with plenty, and thy presses shall burst out with new wine.

Page of Pentacles

Meaning if upright - Scholar. Someone who is a student or who is bright. Someone analytical and careful, with respect for learning, new ideas and opinions. Order, management. Meeting with a board or committee. Messenger. Results are lack-luster. A child. New ideas. Seeker of knowledge.

Meaning if inverted - Wasteful. A marriage of luxury. Rebelliousness, lack of analysis. People with ideas in opposition.

Unfavorable news. Inconsistencies. Over-cautious, hyper-critical, wasteful.

Knight of Pentacles

Meaning if upright - A methodical man, trustworthy but unimaginative, not creative, lacking drive and ambition. He is patient and hard working. He can accept responsibility and follows orders well. The coming or going of a matter concerning resources.

Meaning if inverted - Irresponsibility, impatience, careless. Resources and affairs seem to be at a standstill. Jealousy, smugness, defending that which is outmoded. Stagnation, unemployment.

Queen of Pentacles

Meaning if upright - Intelligent, thoughtful, creative, good use of talents. At times melancholy and moody, timid, charming. Lack of wisdom or foresight bringing about failure. Service rendered by a woman. Seeking harmony.

Meaning if inverted - Too dependant on others. Neglectful. Fear of failure. Suspicious nature. Not much creative ability. Changeable.

King of Pentacles

Meaning if upright - A business man, banker, or owner of large estates. Reliable, settled, financially gifted. An accomplished mathematician or book keeper. He is solid, steady, and dependable. Practical, ingenious, competent, cautious. Slow to anger. Contentment, domestic harmony. Financial security.

Meaning if inverted - Materialistic, one dimensional. Plodding, routine, prone to ruts. Stubborn. Violent if provoked. Perverse use of talents; a person easy to bribe. Insensitive, dull, lacking drive, vicious, vain, prideful.

WANDS

Wands

Representing energy, opposition, quarrel, business, intellect, labor, spring, childhood.

Ace of Wands

Meaning if upright - Birth, enterprise, invention. New business venture. Birth in the family. A new career. Energy, inspiration. Success. Strength, force, determination. A letter, book, writing. Virility, healing.

Meaning if inverted - Selfishness. Setbacks. False starts, clouded feelings. Lack of tenacity, determination or clear vision. Decadence, ruin, cruelty, tyranny, violence.

With the 3 of Wands - you can handle this situation. With the Page of Swords - you will wake up and make a move. With the King of Wands - a man will be of help to get the ball rolling.

Exo. 16:10 And it came to pass, as Aaron spake unto the whole congregation of the children of Israel, that they looked toward the wilderness, and, behold, the glory of the Lord appeared in the cloud.

2 of-Wands

Meaning if upright - Kind and generous. He waits to see his plans bear fruit. An interest in science. Creative, courage, pensive, melancholy. Good things to come.

Other sources say - Loss of will causes lack of success. Double minded. Goals are not worthwhile. Loss of faith. Sadness, restraint, opposition, pressures, responsibility. Thoughts of a trip. Deciding which path to take. Remember the legend of Alexander the Great who wept because he had no more worlds to conquer.

Meaning if inverted - A good beginning may not bear fruit; impatience. Domination, suffering, sadness, fear.

Isaiah 40:31 But they that wait upon the Lord shall renew their strength; they shall mount up with wings as eagles; they shall run, and not be weary; and they shall walk, and not faint.

Lamentations 3:25 The Lord is good unto them that wait for him, to the soul that seeketh him.

3 of Wands

Meaning if upright - There will be cooperation in business. Business is strong. A good partnership brings success. Practical help from a successful person - trade, commerce, strength, success. Hope, desire, attempt, a wish. Collaboration. Oppositions fades. Waiting to reap the benefits of an enterprise already begun. Waiting for your ship to come in.

Meaning if inverted - There is a tendency to scatter one's energies. Mistakes may be made through carelessness. Business venture may be a disappointment. Caution against pride and arrogance. Weak will, nerves, pride, arrogance. Hard work yields disappointment.

Prov. 10:4 He becometh poor that dealeth with a slack hand: but the hand of the diligent maketh rich.

Pro. 25:25 As cold water to a thirsty soul, so is good news from a far country.

Psalm 128:2 For thou shalt eat the labour of thine hands: happy shalt thou be, and it shall be well with thee.

4 of Wands

Meaning if upright - Job and endeavors prosper. Peace, celebration. Romance, marriage. Refuge. Good luck. A good partnership. Harmony. Social acceptance. Happiness.

Meaning if inverted - Inverted, this card carries much the same meaning but in lesser degree. Peace and harmony. Friends, partners, or family are in agreement.

Other sources say - Obstacles to enterprise. Decadence, snobbishness.

With the Sun card - deep contentment.

Rth. 4:12 And let thy house be like the house of Pharez, whom Tamar bare unto Judah, of the seed which the Lord shall give thee of this young woman. So Boaz took Ruth, and she was his wife.

Romans 15:13 Now the God of hope fill you with all joy and peace in believing, that ye may abound in hope, through the power of the Holy Ghost.

Proverbs 16:7 When a man's ways please the Lord, he maketh even his enemies to be at peace with him.

5 of Wands

Meaning if upright - Competition is strong. Possibility of a lawsuit, quarrel, contention. Obstacles, but you have courage and the willingness to fight. Struggles. Mental agility used as a weapon. Victory after an intense battle. Strife and bickering. Fighting against the odds, but you have the advantage. Other sources say; the outcome is undetermined.

Meaning if inverted - New opportunities. Romance and marriage. Too much generosity may deplete you. The forces of nature are entropy. Breakdowns lead to compromise. Compromise leads to a new business opportunity. Guard against self-centeredness and egotism.

With the 10 of Wands - a long hard row to hoe. Difficult, plodding.

Ecc 4:4 Again, I considered all travail, and every right work, that for this a man is envied of his neighbour. This is also vanity and vexation of spirit. 5 The fool foldeth his hands together, and eateth his own flesh. 6 Better is an handful with quietness, than both the hands full with travail and vexation of spirit.

6 of Wands

Meaning if upright - Good news. Triumph, victory, and success through planning and labor. Advancement, achievement, harmony in relationships. Friends are helpful. Possible journey. This is a firm, stable card. A project carried out. Attempt mixed with hope yields a positive outcome.

Meaning if inverted - The outcome is delayed. A trip is postponed. Bad news may come. A warning not to view another's victory as your loss. The winner may be insolent, make sure it isn't you . Pride in position, riches, or success. Infidelity, treachery, betrayal.

Psa. 47:10 clap your hands, all ye people; shout unto God with the voice of triumph.

Proverbs 29:18 Where there is no vision, the people perish: but he that keepeth the law, happy is he.

7 of Wands

Meaning if upright - There will be stiff competition but you can hold your own. If this card comes up in the past, he has already won the fight; if in the future, this is something he may have to face soon. Victory depends on concentration, energy, courage. Valor yields gains. A good exchange of ideas. You will learn much from the exchange.

Meaning if inverted - The situation that worries you will pass you by. Don't let others take advantage. You must take a stance, make a decision or get pushed back. Patience in the face of disputes and threats strengthen your chances. Perplexity, embarrassment, anxiety, conflict.

With the 5 of Swords and 7 of Swords - fight for your independence.

Psa. 27:3 Though an host should encamp against me, my Heart shall not fear: though war should rise against me, in this I will be confident.

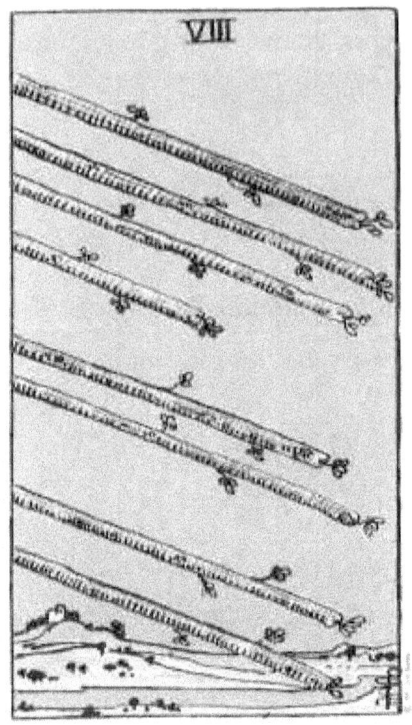

8 of Wands

Meaning if upright - This card indicates speed, quickness, and surprise. It could be a message, idea, or happenings. Journey by air. Love at first, or second sight. Romance. Love of fresh air, gardens, meadows, or sports. Haste, movement, rashness, swiftness. Brilliance wasted on lack of focus.. A private or secret meeting. Only partial success. A sudden occurrence. An epiphany.

Meaning if inverted - Jealousy, fights, quarrels, domestic disputes. The message is late or does not arrive. You must renegotiate later. Courage and boldness with rash action. Anxiety, misgivings, interrogation.

With Knight of Swords - things will happen quickly. Get ready.

Exo. 12:11 And thus shall ye eat it; with your loins girded, your shoes on your feet, and your staff in your hand; and ye shall eat it in haste...

9 of Wands

Meaning if upright - Preparedness yields a hard won victory. Fighting must be done. Strength in defense. Good health. Strength in reserve. A tendency to be stubborn and obstinate. Teaching, planning, preaching, journalist, editor. A confrontation won, but at a cost.

Other sources say - A bad card. Being attacked. Someone is laying in wait.

Meaning if inverted – Warning: you are unprepared for the fight that will come. Refusal to fight for what is right leaves order in ruin. In the battle between good and evil, evil may win if good hesitates or holds back at all. Weakness of character; ill health. Giving in to adversity will bring defeat and possible disaster. Emotions debilitate if not controlled. Threats and mishaps.

I Pe. 5:8 Be sober, be vigilant; because your adversary the devil, as a roaring lion, walketh about, seeking whom he may devour:

Titus 3: 8-11 (The Message Bible) I want you to put your foot down. Take a firm stand on these matters so that those who have put their trust in God will concentrate on the essentials that are good for everyone. Stay away from mindless, pointless quarreling over genealogies and fine print in the law code. That gets you nowhere. Warn a quarrelsome person once or twice, but then be done with him. It's obvious that such a person is out of line, rebellious against God. By persisting in divisiveness he cuts himself off.

10 of Wands

Meaning if upright - Carrying a heavy or oppressive load, either mentally or physically. His heart is heavy with responsibility or pain of emotion. Ruin, disruption, and failure. Burdened, but the goal will be reached. Problems will be solved. Power not regulated. Deceit, lies, guilt, malice, treachery. Putting emphasis on unimportant things. Rest is still a time away.

Other sources say - Confidence, security, honor, and good faith.

With 9 of Swords following - Success is stopped or lawsuits lost.

Meaning if inverted - Strong-arm tactics. Selfish ends. Jealousy, revenge, a desire to ruin others. Someone will try to shift the blame. Treachery, underhandedness. Law suits lost unless prepared.

Mat 11:28 Come unto me, all ye that labor and are heavy laden, and I will give you rest.

Psalm 9:9 The Lord also will be a refuge for the oppressed, a refuge in times of trouble.

Psalm 119:134 Deliver me from the oppression of man: so will I keep thy precepts.

Page of Wands

Meaning if upright - Bright, courageous person. Quick temper. Sudden in the proclamation of love or hate. He has great enthusiasm and a dynamic personality. A message approaches. Ambitious, theatrical, histrionic, shallow, manipulative, domineering. A brother or friend talks about you. A benevolent stranger, pleasure, satisfaction. A childlike delight about a message. Lasting joy comes only from within.

Meaning if inverted - Same meaning as if upright. If the person being read is a woman, her heart may be broken by a rash or selfish man. There may be bad news. Indecisions. Cruelty, slander.

With the King of Wands - you can expect reliability from your support system. If followed by the Page of Cups; a dangerous rival.

Knight of Wands

Meaning if upright - A sudden, rash nature. A man both generous and hasty. Conflict and rivalry. Possible journey or change of residence. The quick coming or going of a matter. Fierce, prideful, impulsive nature. Ready to do battle. A surprising message. Hasty trip.

Meaning if inverted - Fights, discord, no harmony. Interruptions, disruptions. Jealousy, brutality. Narrow-mindedness, suspicion.

Journey delayed. Division, frustration. Quarrel, cruelty, bigotry, alienation.

Queen of Wands

Meaning if upright - A country life, fond of nature, home, family, and gardens. Growth, health, warmth. Down to earth and honorable. Sound judgments. If the card around this one is a man, the reading could involve a relationship. Business success. Worry over a problem. Snobbery, stubborn, vengeful, domineering, unfaithful. Passion, gossip, flirt, meddlesome, fickle.

Meaning if inverted - Strict, stubborn, domineering, controlling, jealous, and revengeful nature. Deceit and infidelity are suggested. Aloof, cool, not easily moved emotionally. Deceit, infidelity.

King of Wands

Meaning if upright - Country, married, fatherly. Passionate, generous, strong, and hasty. Leadership. Quick thinker. Honest, ardent, proud. Endurance, shrewd. Pharisaic. Clergy, preacher, priest, master. The successful crossing of a boundary. The completion of an enterprise, compensation is now expected.

Meaning if inverted - Severe, unyielding, strict. Tends not to change his mind even when he knows he is wrong. Intolerant and prejudiced. Opposition, quarrel, cruelty, sadism.

CUPS

CUPS

Representing love, the heart, romance, emotions, marriage, birth

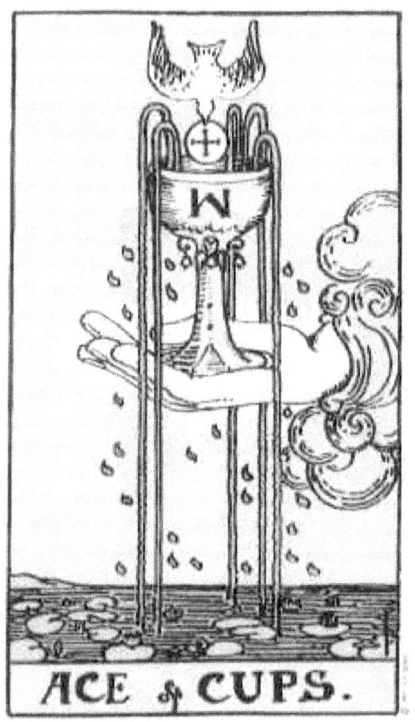

Ace of Cups

Meaning if upright - New starts, new beginnings. Romance and marriage, joy, health, spirituality. Sex, fertility, birth. Pleasure, positive emotions. Intuition, instinct. Change, idealism, enthusiasm. Unrequited love. Your cup overflows with emotions. Love. A bright new day.

Meaning if inverted - Emotions locked up inside. Love unanswered. Feelings pushed to the back. Romance must wait. Distrust of emotions. Selfish, materialism, egotism. False starts.

With the Wheel of Fortune card - happy romance and marriage or affair.

Num. 11:25 And the Lord came down in a cloud, and spake unto him.

ROM 5:5 And hope maketh not ashamed; because the love of God is shed abroad in our hearts by the Holy Ghost which is given unto us.

2 of Cups

Meaning if upright - The beginning of romance or friendship. Synergy between two partners. Harmony, cooperation, spiritual union. Joy, love, things of the heart. Understanding, sympathy, marriage, romance, springtime. Quid pro quo. Domestic harmony. Good health.

Meaning if inverted - Loss of balance. Relationship stressed. Anger, violence, passion. Emotions gone amuck. Love turned to hate. A misunderstanding with someone you care for. Obstacles in love or friendship. Divorce, separation, lust, disagreement, estrangement.

EXO 33:11 And the LORD spake unto Moses face to face, as a man speaketh unto his friend. And he turned again into the camp: but his servant Joshua, the son of Nun, a young man, departed not out of the tabernacle.

PRO 17:17 A friend loveth at all times, and a brother is born for adversity.

3 of Cups

Meaning if upright - Friendship, partnership, romance, celebration, or marriage. A good and happy outcome. The talents in music or painting yet unrealized. Sensitive and sympathetic to others. A party or gathering. Victory, healing, pleasure, luxury, excess. Sex, drugs, rock and roll. Buying something just because you want it. Dancing. Pleasures of the flesh. Bounty.

Meaning if inverted - Pleasure turns to pain. Excess, debauchery. Gossip. Talents lie hidden. Overindulgence in food and drink. Need, want, bills. Watch your money. Don't spend too much on parties.

Ecc. 8:15 Then I commended mirth, because a man hath no better thing under the sun, than to eat, and to drink, and to be merry...

Ecclesiastes 4:12 And if one prevail against him, two shall withstand him; and a threefold cord is not quickly broken.

4 of Cups

Meaning if upright - Dissatisfaction with success or attainment. World-weariness. Emotions turned inward. That which you thought would make you happy, did not. You must now reevaluate. Depression, empty, sad, but kindness and understanding will come from others. Discontent but hesitant to change. The old habits brought you nothing, but now you don't know what to do. Debauchery, luxury, excess, weariness, disgust. New ambitions or goals must be set. Wishing for that which you do not have and ignoring that which you do have.

Meaning if inverted - A new relationship is only possible if you try a new approach. New job, accomplishment, new goals, new ambitions. Going back to school. Training. Beware of obstacles of the heart.

Ecc. 1:14 I have seen all works that are under the sun; and behold, all is vanity and vexation of spirit.

Ecc. 2:11 Then I looked on all the works that my hands has wrought, and on the labor that I had labor to do: and, behold, all was vanity and vexation of spirit, and there was no profit under the sun.

Song 2:5 Stay me with flagons, comfort me with apples: for I am sick of love.

Ecclesiastes 5:10 He that loveth silver shall not be satisfied with silver; nor he that loveth abundance with increase: this is also vanity.

5 of Cups

Meaning if upright - It is more than a minor loss. It is being on a divergent path. This is not what I wanted. It is not what I planned. Like a shoe of the wrong size, it covers and protects but it is not quite right. Not only a partial loss, but an incomplete gain. Not what was hoped for. Not what was planned. Sorrow. Loss of a loved one. A marriage seems on the point of breaking up. The person being read refuses to turn and see the Cups behind him still full of promise. Disillusionment, regret but with something still remaining. Depression, gloom, lonely, sad.

Meaning if inverted - The return of hope and new alliances. The return of an old friend or romance. Courage to overcome difficulties.

With the Sun card - A chance at a deep and powerful romance and marriage. With the 2 of Swords - a relationship is only wasting your energy and time.

Even though he was king and owned most of the kingdom, Ahab wanted the small vineyard that was next to his castle. He wanted it so much that he refused to eat. Eventually his wife, Jezebel, lied and killed for it

I Ki 21:1-10   1 And it came to pass after these things, that Naboth the Jezreelite had a vineyard, which was in Jezreel, hard by the palace of Ahab king of Samaria. 2 And Ahab spake unto Naboth, saying, Give me thy vineyard, that I may have it for a garden of herbs, because it is near unto my house: and I will give thee for it a better vineyard than it; or, if it seem good to thee, I will give thee the worth of it in money. 3 And Naboth said to Ahab, The Lord forbid it me, that I should give the inheritance of my fathers unto thee. 4 And Ahab came into his house heavy and displeased because of the word which Naboth the Jezreelite had spoken to him: for he had said, I will not give thee the inheritance of my fathers. And he laid him down upon his bed, and turned away his face, and would eat no bread. 5 But Jezebel his wife came to him, and said unto him, Why is thy spirit so sad, that thou eatest no bread? 6 And he said unto her, Because I spake unto Naboth the Jezreelite, and said unto him, Give me thy vineyard for money; or else, if it please thee, I will give thee another vineyard for it: and he answered, I will not give thee my vineyard. 7 And Jezebel his wife said unto him, Dost thou now govern the kingdom of Israel? arise, and eat bread, and let thine heart be merry: I will give thee the vineyard of Naboth the Jezreelite. 8 So she wrote letters in Ahab's name, and sealed them with his seal, and sent the letters unto the elders and to the nobles that were in his city, dwelling with Naboth. 9 And she wrote in the letters, saying, Proclaim a fast, and set Naboth on high among the people: 10 And set two men, sons of Belial, before him, to bear witness against him, saying, Thou didst blaspheme God and the king. And then carry him out, and stone him, that he may die.

6 of Cups

Meaning if upright - Someone from your past returns. Memories of fond times, flashback. Pleasant memories. The meaning may also refer to a new friendship or a gift from an admirer. New opportunities. Possibility of a gift or an inheritance. Friendships, old friends.

Meaning if inverted - Pharisaic. Military outlook, Clinging to outworn modes. Living in the past. Friendship that is demanding too much from you and should be discarded. A disappointing relationship.

Pro. 18:24 A man that hath friends must shew himself friendly: and there is a friend that sticks closer that a brother.

7 of Cups

Meaning if upright - An imagination that has been working overtime. It is all in your head. The relationship is not as deep as you hope. Indulgence in dreams. Escapism. A Walter Mitty illusion, indecision. Not knowing what you want.

Meaning if inverted - A good use of will power. A project or path will be selected. Aims realized. A small success.

Psa. 18:11 He made darkness his secret place; his pavilion round about him were dark waters and thick clouds of the skies.

8 of Cups

Meaning if upright - Unhappiness, dissatisfaction, or limited success bring decision to try another way. Abandonment of one's present mode of life or employment. Disappointment in romance or marriage brings separation or another path. Depression and sadness without cause. You are so focused on what has been lost that you let spoil what still remains. An urge to leave, run away. Rejection of materialism in lieu of spiritualism. A spiritual journey. Climbing higher. Going into an unknown realm.

Meaning if inverted - A search for pleasure in worldly things. Overly interested in success. Happiness is being sought, possibly in the wrong places. A new romance about to be discovered. A warning that the things of the world will fade. It is best to seek spiritual pleasures.

With the Sun card - turn back to your spiritual roots.

Gen 12:1 Now the Lord had said to Abram, Get thee out of thy country, and from thy kindred, and from thy father's house, unto a land that I will shew thee: and I will make of thee a great nation...

Ephesians 4:20-25 20 But ye have not so learned Christ;
21 If so be that ye have heard him, and have been taught by him, as the truth is in Jesus :22 That ye put off concerning the former conversation the old man, which is corrupt according to the deceitful lusts; 23 And be renewed in the spirit of your mind; 24 And that ye put on the new man, which after God is created in righteousness and true holiness. 25 Wherefore putting away lying, speak every man truth with his neighbor: for we are members one of another.

9 of Cups

Meaning if upright - As the old saying goes, "fat and happy". Wealth. Material success. Good health. An affair. Pleasures. For now, you feel as if you have all that you need. A wish granted; contentment.

Meaning if inverted - A lack of resources or money. Failure, but not for good. Overindulgence, debauchery. There may be illness or emotional unrest. Mistakes.

With the Fool card - surprise, you'll be secure and happy.

Isa. 58:8 Then shall thy light break forth as the morning, and thine health shall spring forth speedily...

Isaiah 58:11 And the Lord shall guide thee continually, and satisfy thy soul in drought, and make fat thy bones: and thou shalt be like a watered garden, and like a spring of water, whose waters fail not.

10 of Cups

Meaning if upright - Balance reached. Ideas sustained. Relationships sweet; money not strained. The heart's desire attained. Happy family life. Domesticity.

Meaning if inverted - A family quarrel, loss of friendships, betrayal. Some damage may be done to the home. Lust, waste, debauchery.

Ecc. 10:19 A feast is made for laughter, and wine maketh merry; but money answereth all things.

Page of Cups

Meaning if upright - Gentleness, sweetness, kindness, but beware of weakness. Interest in the arts. Dreamy or childish, yet courageous when courage is needed. News, perhaps the birth of a child. Studious, thoughtful, imaginative. New methods, systems, or ideas. A message. Artistic expression.

Meaning if inverted - Selfishness, love of luxury. Someone spoiled. Not much imagination. Someone who takes more than they give. Obstacles, deceptions. Escape through shallow romance.

Knight of Cups

Meaning if upright - Intelligence. A romantic dreamer. He is skilled in the arts, a musician, a poet. The coming or going of a matter involving the emotions. Invitation. A message coming. Playing on the emotions.

Meaning if inverted - Beware of deception or fraud. Sensuality, laziness, idleness, a liar. His imagination runs away with him.

With the 10 of Cups - You are unsure of romance. The intentions of the one you are seeing are questionable

Queen of Cups

Meaning if upright - More feeling and imagination than common sense. A loving family. A good wife and loving mother. Poetic, dreamy, kind. Someone only concerned with their own and not willing to give much help to others. Happiness, pleasure, good-natured. Romance and marriage.

Meaning if inverted - She is a dreamer. She lacks common sense at times. Her imagination has run away with her. A woman that can be selfish or perverse. Not reliable. Pleasure or happiness turned against her.

King of Cups

Meaning if upright - Paternity. A man of art, law, medicine, or divinity. Someone kind and giving. Someone willing to take responsibility for others in a fatherly sense.. He is interested in the arts and sciences. He is calm on the outside and emotional on the inside. A decision in your favor. Watch this one... his emotions surface when unexpected. Wisdom of the heart. Peace.

Meaning if inverted - A liar, crafty, violent. Scandal, injustice, betrayal.

How To Use A Deck of Playing Cards

The standard fifty-two card playing deck of the U.S. and U.K. is the result of an evolution and adaptation of the ancient Tarot. This is a point of information that seems to shock those people who feel uncomfortable with the Tarot but still love to gamble or play card games. Without going into much detail, the sequence of events can be seen very clearly when it is explained that the powerful Major Arcana of the Tarot was dropped to better accommodate parlor games and the names of the suits changed in time and with the migration to the different regions of the world as the cards spread westward.

To see the obvious transition from Tarot to playing cards, let's look at various decks in the Western world and their makeup.

The Tarot deck contains 78 cards with the suits of Cups, Swords, Pentacles (also called disk or coins), and Wands (also called batons or staves).

The Italian deck of playing cards contains forty cards consisting of Cups, Staves, Coins, and Swords. The Spanish deck contains fifty-two cards with the same suits as the Italian deck.

The French deck is made up of fifty-two cards divided into Hearts, Trefoils, Tiles, and Spades or Pike Heads.

The U.S. and U.K. decks contain fifty-two cards. The suits are Hearts, Clubs, Spades, and Diamonds.

Keeping in mind the Major Arcana is missing, and the Court Cards have undergone a slight transition, the rest can be seen in a series of adaptations and translations as the cards moved from country to country. Swords were renamed Spades. The names say it all with the sharp, warlike quality and meaning remaining intact.

Staves or Batons were renamed Clubs. This is just a matter of word choice more than anything. These two changes can be understood easily, and could have occurred in simple translation preferences as the cards moved into different languages and countries.

The change from Coin or Disk into Diamonds is less of a translation phenomena and more of a cultural shift. A thing of value, the Coin, is usurped by another item of worth, but with a more lasting quality, the Diamond. The interpretation of money or value follows both.

The last change is more complicated. How the Cup became the Heart can seen in the meaning of the suit of Cups as a whole. In the Tarot, the suit of Cups stands for emotion and love, in other words, the things of the heart. As was mentioned in the history section, there were cards made in the thirteenth and fourteenth centuries which had Hearts in place of Cups. The bridge between the two suits has to do with the idea of the "loving cup" or an emotional icon representing love. Thus, Cups became Hearts.

Keeping in mind the existence of playing cards predate the Tarot by a short period of time, we have already established a relationship of evolution between types of playing cards and the Tarot. Even though the Tarot was composed in the soul of feudal Christianity, and the Tarot's Court Cards mimic the society of the time, one may still apply the modern meanings of certain cards in fortune telling and adapt them to a deck of cheaper and more available playing cards. The information below is but one set of meanings imposed on playing cards for the purpose of using them to foretell the future.

General Meaning of Playing Cards

The number of the cards represents a number of time periods. An ace would be the number one, one day, week, month or year. A 2 card would represent 2 days, weeks, months, or years, or simply the number 2, and so forth. The number can also indicate a date of time, such as 2 o'clock or February 2nd. You must rely on the question and the other cards and use your intuition to ferret out the meaning of these detail.

ACE
3 Aces together means a wish will come true. Good luck. A bright event. 4 Aces together means a blessing. A wish is guaranteed. Something good is very near. Ace of Spades reversed- death, divorce, total separation.

TWO
Two children. The second child. A two year old. An event happens soon. 2 of Spades- separation. 2 of Spades with an Ace of Spades- separation, a break of a relationship, death.

THREE
3 of Spades with a 7 of Spades and 8 of Spades - sickness, sick sex, homosexuality, abuse, sadomasochism. 3 of Spades with a face card -

someone is worried. 3 of Hearts- Bright and good card. 3 of Diamonds- happy, good luck. 3 of Diamonds with the 4 of Diamonds - a gift. Jewelry. Something shiny. 3 threes - a sexual encounter.

FOUR

Change. 4 of Hearts or Diamonds - things bright and good. With two 4's- A change of doors, residence, schedule, work, or position. With four 4's- An unavoidable change. A definite change. A great restructuring.

FIVE

Moment of change, travel.

SIX

Two red 6's with a black 6 - things get better. A reversal of trouble. Taking control of your life again. Two black 6's with a red 6 - trouble. Someone has too much control over you or wishes to harm you.

SEVEN

Three or more 7's- A period of time. Seven days, weeks, or months. Someone seven years old. 7 of Clubs- A child. A pregnancy. If the majority of the cards surrounding it are black then the child will be a boy, if red then the child is a girl. Two black 7's - Accident, mishap. Three 7's - Good luck, a wish. Four 7's - a period of time, seven days, weeks, or months. 7 with 8 of Spades- Legal or medical. 7 with an 8 - blue collar worker. Someone who works with their hands.

EIGHT

Two 8's- Out of town, long distance, a phone call long distance, a visit with someone who lives out of town. Three 8's- Good luck. A turn of events. Four 8's- Birth, pregnancy. Relating to a pregnant woman. 8 of Spades with a 7 of Spades- Legal, medical, court, jail, doctor's office, post office, bank.

NINE

Two 9's - A period of time. Three 9's - Something hoped for will come to pass. Four 9's - Something will be remembered. September. Nine months.

TEN

A period of time, the tenth month, ten o'clock. A ten year old. Three 10's - A gift. Winning. Unexpected money, but not a great amount. 10 of Hearts - Marriage. The card falling next to it will tell the number of times they will be or have been married.

JACK

A young, single male. Two Jacks – Friendships. Jack of Hearts - A sweetheart or lover. Two Kings with a Jack - Someone in uniform. Three Jacks - Out of the state or country.

QUEEN

Female, mother, grandmother, home. Three Queens - Gossip, talk, news spreads fast. Four Queens - A meeting of women such as a club. Queen with a 7 of Clubs - The woman represented by the Queen is pregnant.

KING

A male person, father, authority. Two Kings with a Jack - Someone in uniform. Authority, police, armed forces, guard, doctor, nurse. Three Kings - Money, prosperity, inheritance, legal papers, winnings. Four Kings - A meeting with someone in high places or an authority. Someone held in esteem.

Meaning of Each Playing Card

Hearts

Cups – Water – Love - Religion

Ace of Hearts – Love and happiness. The home, a love letter. This card is a particularly favourable card that indicates troubles and problems lifting.

2 of Hearts – A warm partnership or engagement. This is a very favourable card that indicates strength and support coming from a partner.

3 of Hearts – Love and happiness when the entire spread is generally favourable. In a difficult spread, this can indicate emotional problems and an inability to decide who to love.

4 of Hearts – Travel, change of home or business.

5 of Hearts – Jealousy; some ill-will from people around you.

6 of Hearts – A sudden wave of good luck. Someone takes care of you, takes warm interest in you.

7 of Hearts – Someone whose interest in you is unreliable; someone with fickle affections for you. This card can indicate lovesickness.

8 of Hearts – An unexpected gift or visit; an invitation to a party.

9 of Hearts – The card of wishes. A wish/dream fulfilled. Look to the card just preceding this one to determine what the querent desires.

10 of Hearts – Good luck, success. This is an important card that suggests good fortune after difficulty.

Jack of Hearts – A warm-hearted friend. A fair-haired youth; or a young person with Water signs predominating in his or her chart. Often this points to a younger admirer.

Queen of Hearts – A fair-haired woman with a good nature; or a woman with Water signs predominating in her chart. Kind advice. Affectionate, caring woman. Sometimes, this card can indicate the mother or a mother figure.

King of Hearts – A fair-haired man with a good nature; or a man with Water signs predominating in his chart. Fair, helpful advice. Affectionate, caring man. This man helps you out without much talk. His actions reveal his kindness and concern.

Clubs

Wands – Fire – Toil

Ace of Clubs – Wealth, prosperity, unexpected money/gain. However, in a difficult spread, this money may disappear almost as quickly as it appears.

2 of Clubs – Obstacles to success; malicious gossip.

3 of Clubs – Love and happiness; successful marriage; a favorable long-term proposition. A second chance, particularly in an economical sense.

4 of Clubs – Beware of dishonesty or deceit; avoid blind acceptance of others at this time.

5 of Clubs – New friendships, alliances are made.

6 of Clubs – Financial aid or success.

7 of Clubs – Business success, although there may be problems with the opposite sex. A change in business that may have been expected or earned, such as a promotion.

8 of Clubs – Work/business problems that may have to do with jealousy. This is generally thought to be quite unfavorable.

9 of Clubs – Achievement; sometimes a wealthy marriage or a sudden windfall.

10 of Clubs – Business success. Good luck with money. A trip taken now may result in a new friend or love interest.

Jack of Clubs – A dark-haired or fiery youth. Popular youth who is good-hearted and playful. Can also indicate an admirer.

Queen of Clubs – Dark-haired, confident woman; or a woman with Fire predominating in her chart. She may give you good advice.

King of Clubs – Dark-haired, kind-hearted man; or a man with Fire predominating in his chart. A generous and spirited man.

Spades

Sword – Air – Conflict

Ace of Spades – Misfortune; sometimes associated with death or, more often, a difficult ending.

2 of Spades – Breaks in relationships; deceit. A break in an important process in the seeker's life. If the question concerns a particular romantic interest, this is considered a warning card – infidelity or separation is quite likely.

3 of Spades – Breaks in relationships. Sometimes indicates that a third person is breaking into a relationship somehow.

4 of Spades – Small worries, problems. Financial difficulties, personal lows.

5 of Spades – Opposition and obstacles that are temporary; a blessing in disguise. Sometimes indicates a negative or depressed person.

6 of Spades – Small changes and improvements.

7 of Spades – Advice that is best not taken; loss. There is some obstacle to success, and this indicates that obstacles may be coming from within the seeker.

8 of Spades – Temptation, misfortune, danger, upsets.

9 of Spades – Illness, accident, bad luck. The seeker is at his/her personal low.

10 of Spades – Worry; bad news.

Jack of Spades – A youth who is hostile or jealous.

Queen of Spades – Widowed or divorced woman; or a woman with Air predominating in her chart.

King of Spades – Dark-haired man; or a man with Air predominating in his chart. An ambitious man, perhaps self-serving.

Diamonds

Pentacles – Earth – Business - Money

Ace of Diamonds – Change; a message, often about money, and usually good news.

2 of Diamonds – A business partnership; a change in relationship; gossip.

3 of Diamonds – A legal letter. Be tactful with others in order to avoid disputes.

4 of Diamonds – Financial upswing; an older person may give good advice.

5 of Diamonds – Happiness and success. A change for the better. A birth, or good news for a child. This is a good time to start new projects.

6 of Diamonds – Relationship problems, arguments. Separation.

7 of Diamonds – An argument concerning finances, or on the job. Generally expected to be resolved happily.

8 of Diamonds – New job; change in job situation. The young or the old may find love on a trip.

9 of Diamonds – A new business deal; travel; restlessness; a change of residence.

10 of Diamonds – A change in financial status, often for the better.

11 Jack of Diamonds – A youth, possibly in uniform or, a jealous person who may be unreliable. A person who brings news, generally negative, but relatively minor.

12 Queen of Diamonds – A fair-haired woman; or a woman with Earth predominating in her chart. A gossip.

13 King of Diamonds – A fair-haired or graying man, or a man with Earth predominating in his chart. A man of authority, status, or influence.

The Joker

The Joker is the only card remaining from the Tarot trumps. He corresponds to The Fool in the Tarot deck. The Joker represents choices, folly, something unexpected and uncontrolled can occur. Some decks have two jokers but in a reading only one should be used.

Combinations of Playing Cards

Ace of Diamonds/Ten of Hearts – romance leading to marriage

Ace of Diamonds/Ten of Diamonds – marriage for money

Ace of Diamonds/Six of Hearts – invitation

Ace of Diamonds/Six of Spades – news of failure

Ace of Diamonds/Seven of Hearts – news of rivalry

Ace of Diamonds/Nine of Hearts – love letter

Ace of Clubs among Diamonds – success in money matters, business deal

Several Court cards – a social gathering

King, Queen or Jack between two cards of same number – support for person

King or Queen between two Jacks – protection from enemies

Queen of Spades between a King and a Queen – relationship break-up

Jack next to either King or Queen – protection

Jack among several Diamonds – message about money

Seven, Ten and Three of Diamonds – a secret wish will come true

Seven and Eight of Diamonds – do not give cause for or spread gossip, will come back to you

Eight of Diamonds and several Court cards of any suit – a social gathering

Eight and Nine of Spades (or Nine and Ten of Spades) – health problems

Nine and Ten of Diamonds – journey by sea

Nine of Diamonds/Eight of Hearts – journey for pleasure

Ten of Diamonds/Ten of Clubs – windfall

Ten of Diamonds/Eight of Clubs – meaningful journey

Ten of Hearts/King & Queen of Hearts – possible wedding

Ten of Diamonds/Seven of Spades – delays

Five and Eight of Spades – jealous rival, be careful

Four of Diamonds and Four of Spades – a decision against one's will

Multiples of Cards – If Two or More of Certain Cards Appear

Ace – Beginnings, Partnerships, reunions, marriage

2 - oppositions, breakups, a crossroad 2 2s bring breakups

3 - Choice, hope, creative

4 - Foundations laid, 2 4s or 3 4s brings a shaky foundation

5 - change, challenges, 3 5s brings disappointment

6 – harmony, adaptation, 2 6s or 4 6s brings challenges with family or friends

7 - surprises or conspiracy. With 7 of hearts and diamonds there is love and pleasure.

8 - getting what is deserved, indiscretion, worries, burdens

9 – Fortune, gains, good health

10 – completion, improvement, success. With 3 10s plans get upset.

Jacks – a young male or female. 2 or 3 jacks bring fights or false friends

Queens – Mature female, 2 queens meeting with a friend, 3 queens bring betrayal

Kings – mature male, business, politics, support, success

Meaning of Symbols in the Tarot Cards

If Something Catches Your Eye

The cards have been shuffled and laid out. The reading has begun. The reader first looks over the entire 14 card spread for the sense of a pattern or flow to the cards. If there is anything within a card that catches the reader's attention he or she should take note of it and check the list below for a general meaning of that symbol.

Angel - The call of your higher nature. Guidance. Armor, warfare, battle, readiness.

B - Boaz - Grace, unmerited favor. Redemption, protection. Balance, judgment, equality, quantifying, qualifying.

Black - Depression, distress, tension, emptiness, evil.

Blindfold - Helplessness. Held hostage by a person or a situation. Seeking inner truth. Look inward.

Blood - Life force. Vitality. Harm. Murder. Death, sacrifice.

Cat - Feminine nature, occult. Finicky, allof.

Censor - Dispersing or containing the prayers and purification. Incense. Spiritual force.

Chains – Slavery, bondage, weighted down, restrained from actions or movement.

Circle - Eternity. Cycles. Recurrence. Also protection or entrapment. Inclusion within the circle. Exclusion of those outside the circle.

Cloud - Storms, chaos, unknown, misfortune. Coming wind or rain in life.

Crawfish - The two sides of the unconscious mind. Unpredictable, intuition. Conclusion is counter to logic.

Cross - Self sacrifice. Purification. Spiritual awakening. Surrendering ego to see the truth and attain enlightenment.

Crown - Leadership, authority, power, command, royalty.

Crutch - Lack of wholeness. Sickness. Dependence on something or someone. The feeling you are incapable of achieving a goal.

Cup - Love, heart, female, emotions. Fullness, emptiness. Subconscious, clergy, intuition.

Devil - Deceiver, entrapment, enslaver. Evil person or situation. The situation has a cost. The trap you think you are in is an illusion. To escape simply walk away.

Dog – Depending on the disposition of the dog - Guardian, faithful, animal nature, dogs of war, hounds of hell, to be dogged and pursued. Friendly, playful. Vicious, attack.

Dove - Peace, spiritual inspiration. Holy Spirit. Mild and calm spirit.

Falcon - Control, thought, mind, speed, the ability to attack.

Fire - Destruction, removal, purification.

Fish - Christianity. Food, substance.

Garland or wreath - Victory, celebration, reward.

Hammer - Craftsmanship. Forging or making something. Force molds situations.

Hoe - Hard work, tending, overseeing, attentiveness.

J - Jacob - Law, judgment, guilt.

Lantern - Inner and outer illumination, searching, instruction, wisdom.

Lion - Power, authority, control. Fierce protection of attack.

Marsh or mud - Uncertainty, deception, unclearness. A difficult journey. Energy yields few results

Moon - Female, illusive, intuition. Things hidden. Subconscious.

Pillar - Phallic, strong, supportive.

Pomegranates - Fertility, fruitfulness, a female sign.

Rainbow - Promise, hope, happiness.

Scepter – Authority, rule, command.

Salamander - Renewal, regeneration, hope, hidden potential or situation.

Snake - The lower nature of man. Lies, a type of worldly wisdom. Danger from unexpected places.

Sun or sunflower - Fertility, joy, harmony. Birth, life.

Sun rays - Healing energy. Life force.

Sword - Punishment, protection. Male force, war, battle.

Tara or Torah - Wisdom, divine knowledge, learning. Word of direction from God.

Wand - The portal between mind and manifestation. Energy, spirituality, inspiration, determination, strength, intuition, creativity, ambition and expansion, original thought.

Water - Water can sustain a ship, water can sink it. Spirit, female, intuition, subconscious mind.

Wheel - Change, cycles, fate.

Yod - Life force. Spirit

1 (ACE) - Beginnings, starts, birth.

2 - Reciprocity, harmony, disharmony, union, divided, duality, partnership.

3 - Creativity, social, relationships, fertility.

4 - Foundations, logic, material world, limitations.

5 - Change, activity, conflict, quixotic, unpredictable.

6 - Family, dependability, judgment and protection in a parental sense.

7 - Maturation, perfection, completion, intuition.

8 - Justice, law, balanced forces, defamation.

9 - Cycles end, paths completed, endings, preparation for the journey, emotions.

10 - Power or strength in good or bad. If negative there is a solitary or abandoned feeling.

Conclusion

To truly understand a concept, theory, idea, or invention, one must know and comprehend its origin, history, and evolution. How and why something changes explains the impact of the environment and conditions shaping it. This is true for living organisms and is not any less significant for the Tarot cards.

As we explored the origin of the cards in twelth century Europe, we saw how society implanted its mark on the Tarot - applying the values and makup of society with its kings and courts; as well as the Christian beliefs of the day. In addition, we learned that the established influence of the Bible, art, astrology, and Kabala found their ways into the cards. We have seen a "full-circle-transfer" from the creation of playing cards, to the Tarot as a type of card game, and finally to the application of Tarot card meanings to the common deck of playing cards. It is clear how the church's acceptence of the cards followed the King's decrees. We speculated on how the decrees followed the flow of cash in gambling. Finally, we gained insight into the symbols used in the cards.

The Tarot has been with us for over 500 years. The cards encompass the art, histroy, feelings, and thoughts of countless generations. To become acquainted with them will enrich our lives.

Tarot: The History, Meaning, and Use of the Cards   by *Anne Burton*

BIBLIOGRAPHY

DICTIONARY OF THE TAROT BY BILL BUTLER PUBLISHED BY SCHOCKEN BOOKS NEW YORK. COPYRIGHT 1975

THE ELEMENTS OF THE TAROT BY A.T. MANN PUBLISHED BY SHAFTESBURY, DORSET ROCKPORT, MASS COPYRIGHT 1993

DOWN TO EARTH TAROT BY ALAN STEWARD PUBLISHED BY ABACO PUBLISHING CO. BIRMINGHAM, AL. COPYRIGHT 1992

TAROT MADE EASY BY NANCY GAREN PUBLISHED BY FIRESIDE BOOKS NEWYORK. COPYRIGHT 1989

THE TAROT READER BY NANCY SHAVICK PUBLISHED BY BERKLY BOOKS NEW YORK. COPYRIGHT 1991

TAROT IN TEN MINUTES BY R.T. KASER PUBLISHED BY AVON BOOKS DRESDEN, TN. COPYRIGHT 1989

THE PICTORIAL KEY TO THE TAROT BY ARTHUR EDWARD WAITE PUBLISHED BY U.S.GAMES INC. STANFORD, CT. COPYRIGHT 1910

FORTUNE TELLING BY TAROT CARDS BY SASHA FENTON

PUBLISHED BY AQUARIAN PRESS, WELLINGBOROUGH NORTHAMPTONSHIRE GREAT BRITIAN COPYRIGHT 1985

THE COMPLETE GUIDE TO THE TAROT BY EDEN GRAY PUBLISHED BY BANTAM BOOKS NEW YORK COPYRIGHT 1972

Illustrations from the Rider-Waite Tarot Deck (R), known also as the Rider Tarot and the Waite Tarot, reproduced by permission of U.S. Games Systems, Inc., Stamford, Ct. 06902 USA. Copyright © 1971 by U.S. Games and Systems, Inc. Further reproduction prohibited. The Rider-Waite Tarot Deck (R) is a registered trademark of U.S. Games Systems, Inc.

Tarot: The History, Meaning, and Use of the Cards   by *Anne Burton*

Tarot: The History, Meaning, and Use of the Cards   by *Anne Burton*

Tarot: The History, Meaning, and Use of the Cards   by *Anne Burton*

www.ingramcontent.com/pod-product-compliance
Lightning Source LLC
Chambersburg PA
CBHW050136170426
43197CB00011B/1856